A3

BRITISH SILVER COINS

SINCE 1816

by

PETER J. DAVIES

with

Engravers' Patterns and Proofs

and

Unofficial Pieces

First Edition *1982*

ISBN *0 9507913 0 X*

Photography and Typography
by Peter J. Davies

Printed in England

CONTENTS

PREFACE

The Romance of English silver coins these past dozen centuries provides unparalleled historical insight into the origin and culture of the British Isles. From conception the remarkable silver coinage of Tower Hill remains unrivalled and although strictly token in value these impressive coins were at once both marvellously inventive and superbly designed.

This reappraisal will hopefully form a definitive study of the last duodecimal English silver coins and their immediate patterns to which the Tower Hill mint was solely devoted. The main consideration has been to emphasise currency coin varieties as no publication has concerned itself too deeply with this important aspect.

The series is tabulated reign by reign and thousands of silver coins have been examined extending the possible eight hundred and ninty-five dated denominations up to almost thirteen hundred different varieties, which represents about three times the number previously published. Three hundred and five cameo photographs depict these variations with over a hundred pairs of type coin illustrations commencing each section. Additionally several hundred proofs and over a hundred and fifty engravers' patterns complete all the known authorised issues producing, in total, about two thousand two hundred catalogued pieces. The checker-board format devotes vertical columns for dates, over-dates and die-pairings with horizontal columns utilising mint-state, proofs and metal differences This new arrangement allows a collector unencumbered vision of currency pieces whilst patterns and proofs are still to hand.

With a century's over production of silver bullion terminating and inevitable rising living standards throughout the world cheap supplies of silver will diminish before the next century. These converging factors in combination with increasing numismatic interest, must ensure any collection however modest, appreciating in value and pleasure during the coming years. The official issues that are catalogued herein will undoubtedly provide an excellent basis for forming a collection of Royal Mint silver coins.

Much information has been received from Mr Ronald Stafford who has practically restructured the whole Victorian young-head series and his assistance is gratefully acknowledged. Thanks are also extended to Mr David Traynor for kindly providing many coins for photography.

INTRODUCTION

Coin Condition

This catalogue only recognises 'mint' and 'F.D.C.' states of preservation for valuation purposes. With twentieth century coins this is generally the only accepted collectable grade and to a great extent for nineteenth century issues. Proof coins will often remain on or near F.D.C., a really worn proof is rarely encountered. 'Mint state' implies the coin is 'as struck' and is issued by the Mint with its original brilliant lustre. This brilliance often is not retained and a choice natural toning becomes equally desirable. 'Uncirculated' describes a mint condition coin, possibly with original lustre, but which would include slight 'bag marking' and minor cabinet friction.

Minting methods have gradually become less careful since this series originated. Pistrucci's tissue wrapped crowns are far removed from the millions of bagged first World War issues hastily produced for troop payments and 'bag marking' is part and parcel of many issues discussed in this handbook. 'Ghosting' – an outline of the obverse portrait traceable on the reverse – appeared after the turn of the century due to unbalanced obverse and reverse reliefs. Periodic reduced striking pressure, conserving dies during shortages, contribute to coins appearing slightly worn yet experiencing no circulation.

Silver coins cannot be successfully cleaned but surface grime can be removed with a clean piled cloth, gently rotating the coin between the cloth and fingers until the original toning is reached, when further pressure may be applied for final buffing. Change cloth to avoid build-up of dirt laundering after each use. Any further cleaning may damage the surface and eventually induce a pewter coloured burnishment. Coins exhibiting striated, often parallel, cleaning lines are classified as damaged. These pieces have been thoughtlessly cleaned with an abrasive agent. Likewise pieces immersed in proprietary cleaning liquids will show a slight yellowish patina replacing the amount of toning removed. These coins are still impaired and this yellow crust becomes more pronounced with time. Washing silver coins should also be avoided. Obvious further damage includes piercing, attempted piercing, mounting, plugging, initialing either visible or erased and enchasing relief detail. Enamelled and gilded pieces are not collectors' items and such treatment is illegal rendering these coins, in law, counterfeit.

Storage can also produce damaging conditions and an inert atmosphere should be favoured. The classic configuration of trays and coin cabinet in mahogany or rosewood give ready access, attractive appearance and protection. Polyvinyl envelopes are best used in conjunction with acetate packets, the coin is then not pressing against the vegetable based outer envelope preventing spores forming verdigris. A worn piece will be more prone to this happening and this 'double glazing' eliminates condensation and any vinyl envelop cracking. Coins are better handled only by the rims and then with grease-free or gloved hands. White paper envelopes often contain chemicals which are harmful to silver coins especially the first debased alloy with its high nickel content and this reaction eventually shows the nickel darkly speckled across the coin's surface. Pieces kept in leather purses for a considerable time also exhibit a dark grey toning and, as always, are better left in this condition.

Coin Valuation

Valuations tabulated in this handbook reflect what a given piece would realise whether offered for sale by collector, dealer or auction house. The finest grade has been selected for valuations and this not only prices individual pieces in the most popular collected grade but despite no catalogue ever being exact, this still forms the best expression of comparative rarity. Also values for lower grade pieces are generally more difficult to determine than mint condition coins where a greater consensus of value exists.

Values of all coins collectively are determined by several factors. Coins of a particular country having a low national product will on the whole tend to attract lower prices than those of countries with high per capita wealth. Trends in international metal prices, especially gold, dictate a large proportion of present-day pricing. A strong silver bullion price will give further impetus for modern issues producing rises through all states of preservation ensuring price minimums even for damaged pieces. At this present time issues between 1816 and 1919 contain about twenty times face-value in silver – having previously touched seventy times – with fine condition crowns minimizing about eight pounds. Silver coins prior to 1947 represent about half these figures. Over the last decade modern silver coins have shown greater increases than many earlier issues and this trend will probably continue. With coins nearer to present day fashionable trends will influence popularity cycles, either short-lived or sustained and a previously neglected series can quickly appreciate in value.

Values of individual coins are determined by availability, desirability and preservation. Small mintages and low retention from previous years create less availability for later collectors. Desirability both encompasses common and rare coins in first-class condition coupled with esthetic appeal, metallic content, size, age and origin. Generally speaking a large coin with equal rarity to a smaller one will be the more valuable. Likewise gold, silver and copper descend in value and importance. Preservation dictates the final worth of any particular coin and many currency issues covered by this handbook formulate very broadly a halving price scale. A coin valued at £100 in mint state would if 'extremely fine' probably be worth rather more than half at about £60. A 'very fine' piece would be about a quarter of mint at £25 and a 'fine' example in the region of one tenth.

The valuations for many rarer pieces are of necessity conservative estimates of what similar pieces would realise if offered at the present time. Where extremely rare coins are permanently within institutions, this academic price caters for subsequent pieces appearing on the market. Likewise prices for previously unpublished varieties listed for the first time are valuations reflecting how a market might consider these varieties once having become established.

No value is maintained, however, if choice coins are misplaced, stolen or damaged and preventing this requires some consideration. Insurance companies will advise on comprehensive policies covering loss, theft and fire. Obviously a steel safe-deposit box kept banked and fully insured provides the minimum of risk suiting most collectors, but should the bank be burgled a comprehensive inventory must separately be kept noting all pertinent details with enlarged photographs of important items.

Die Varieties

The prime concern of this catalogue is to tabulate all principal die variations within this important series. For the collector unconcerned with patterns and proofs and limited funds, varieties add considerable interest to lower grade regular date issues, in fact many unpublished varieties are known only in worn state as several of the illustrations will show. Identifying particular die varieties is relatively simple through the profuse illustrations, each with accompanying descriptions making lower grade coins equally easy to discern. The distinctive feature, illustrated to identify a particular die, is viewed with that portion of the coin facing spectator. Where legend letters are utilised pointing towards the rim, then an imaginary line is extended through the letter upright towards the border beads.

Earlier nineteenth century issues exhibit rather more variation with many coins subject to individual letter strengthening by over-striking. Generally this is hardly discernable but occasionally the double striking can be seen and these along with slight letter tilting and similar deviations would become impractical to list and difficult to distinguish. Dates also vary as the design alone was transfered from master to working dies leaving the date for hand punching, naturally giving rise to different positioning and these expected irregularities are not tabulated. The middle Victorian issues conveniently carry die or registration numbers attesting to the quantity of working dies required for particular years. After 1887 date variations rarely occur and where an obvious difference is encountered these sub-varieties are footnoted. Whilst these date alterations are not regarded as major varieties they often assist confirming further die variations.

Those varieties listed therefore should represent the total number of different master dies prepared for any particular year with exception of size differences. Where a die-pairing is suspected to exist, although unconfirmed, this expectation is denoted symbolically in place of a valuation. Commencing from the last Victorian issue original designs, when pantographically transfered to master dies, occasionally produce slight enlargement or reduction of the exact original design. Usually a particular die-size lasts several years but if within a given year two very noticable die-sizes occur these are classified whereas imperceptable variations are overlooked. When die-size alters in step with the year change these also remain unrecorded.

This handbook allocates many proofs into new catagories relating to die variety and where pieces are unexamined these are assumed to derive from the last die-sinking of that year. This may not always be true and modifications will be needed, perhaps some or all die-pairings occuring proof for that year. Likewise the highest recorded die numbers, where unexamined are presumed to use the last die-pairings of a particular year. Maundy threepence types will be completely identified when all sets have been classified.

Proofs and Patterns

All known proof pieces originating from the Royal Mints are listed and valued. Doubtless more pieces kept in state custody and various sources will, as they surface, be added further to these already mentioned. Many early proofs are plain edged – a tradition from earlier issues – as 'milling' is needed only to protect currency pieces. These highly prized coins represent the quintessence of coiners' art. The term 'proof' describes a method of manufacture where plachet and die-field are highly polished with intaglio portions often acid treated rendering a 'frosted' effect on any raised coin surfaces. Full lists of regular proof sets appear after the coin tables.

By definition pattern pieces remain divorced from currency issues and although thousands are sometimes produced, struck to proof format, these remain unadopted for general circulation. However, if for a given year only a pattern is struck and ultimately currency pieces embrace this design then this complimentary pattern augments the currency tables. Where pieces have no regard for contemporary currency designs these are listed separately under patterns. Although attribution remains difficult currency pieces are always identifiable by their own 'mint state' columns. Only those patterns evidently of official origin and produced by Royal Mint engravers are acknowledged. All other none Royal Mint pieces are only viewed as essays many having no possibility of adoption and few achieving the refinement of Mint issues. A priced listing of these pieces appears directly after the decimal issues.

Trials and Errors

Trial pieces have been omitted from this catalogue due to their incomplete nature. They are interesting being usually struck 'out of metal' by an engraver examining die progress and usually are lead squeezes.

It is suprising that errors are not more widely collected as nearly all are rare and always add interest within a collection. They cover a broad variation and although not within this catalogue's scope do merit some discussion. The simplest error encountered is a 'mis-strike' with the die not centrally striking the blank and leaving an area of the flan and 'milling' partially struck. Other erroneous varieties comprise of coins with thicker or thinner flans, coins struck without a collar and brokages – coins with an identical obverse and reverse but one side being incuse. Errors also occur when coins are struck from different metal blanks the more important when inadvertently struck in a superior metal. Some rare errors are constant die flaws perhaps from 'clashed' or filled-in dies or others date changing puncheons stamped twice producing a double struck effect. Overstriking and 'blundered' die-sinking are not strictly erroneous and where pronounced these have been recorded appropriately in the tables.

Maundy Sets

Listed at the end of each reign are small sets of coins issued every year covered by this catalogue except 1816 and 1821. These sets consist of uniform fourpence, threepence, twopence and penny pieces and are specifically struck for Maundy Thursday in Passion week. This ancient ceremony originates from the 'mandatum' or 'new commandment' of St. John XIII 34. Prior to 1909 these sets could be obtained through banks but following some controversy King Edward VII decreed these coins should only be presented to selected subjects in attendance at the ceremony. In recent years the reigning monarch has distributed these coins with the sovereign's age representing the number of pence given and in turn equivalent to an equal number of male and female recipients.

These little coins although legal tender do not circulate, and being struck to proof standard they readily distinguish themselves from currency threepences and twopences. Often these Maundy sets become richly toned induced a bit from their original leather purses or small unofficial cases. Since decimalisation all Maundy values have represented 'new pence' denominations worth four, three, two and one new pence respectively including apparently currency threepences from 1870.

Grades of Preservation

F.D.C. :	Fleur de Coin :	Perfect unblemished mint state. Generally ascribed to proofs.
	Mint state :	Original 'as struck' condition and virtually perfect.
Unc. :	Uncirculated :	'As issued' including some bag mark grazing.
E.F. :	Extremely fine :	Some scuffing apparent on high points but generally appearing uncirculated.
V.F. :	Very fine :	Wear apparent on prominent surfaces from limited circulation.
F. :	Fine :	Considerable wear but rims and legend quite distinct.
	Fair :	Substantially worn with rims and legend showing some weakness.
	Poor :	Extremely worn and design barely recognisable.

THE DEVELOPMENT OF MODERN BRITISH COINAGE

"I sell here Sir, what all the world desires to have – *power*"

M.Boulton.

The most important influence of all on the origination and construction of modern British coinage if not that of the world, rested with Matthew Boulton F.R.S. a manufacturer of smallwares. Boulton's early life may be of interest to the uninitiated collector. Born on September 3rd, 14th N.S. 1728 he entered during 1745 into business with his father. His first marriage, occasioned in February 1749 at St. Mary's church Lichfield, was to a distant cousin Mary Robinson. A regrettably short marriage as Mary died in 1759 and Boulton remarried, amid moral descension, her sister Anne in Spring 1761 being co-heiress of her father's estate. The following year Boulton formed a partnership with a one John Fothergill and together they built the Soho factory. This name was not the endowment of Boulton but a Shakespearian hunting term taken from a nearby inn-sign depicting a hunting group with the huntsman goading his dogs and the halloo 'so-ho' shown coming from his mouth. The cost of this new site amounted to more than a thousand pounds and his original premises at Snow Hill were enlarged as warehouses.

Upon the 28th of August 1768 Boulton encountered James Watt and a partnership discussed, along with John Roebuck a friend of Boulton who defrayed the cost of the most important patent ever granted. It was for a 'new method of lessening the consumption of steam and fuel in fire-engines' the patent being granted number 913 but when drafting this famous specification Boulton and Dr. Small unfortunately advised Watt incorrectly on two points – the first being an absence of drawings, the second claiming 'a principal of action instead of an application of principal'. Boulton later came by this patent when Roebuck suffered bankrupcy. Nevertheless in 1774 with Watt's engine perfected an immediate partnership was formed between the two ranking as one of the most important in industrial history. In 1785 Boulton instigated the Cornish Metal Company formed with the prime intention of stablising the cost of copper by a price maintenance guaranteed to producers. However, because of the enhanced price of copper and prolific output from the famous Angelsey mines, vast stocks accumulated for which no profitable market could be found. Boulton realised that its use for coinage would solve all the problems.

Boulton's first interest in coinage began when appointed agent to receive dilapidated coins from the public and early in 1772 a letter to Lord Dartmouth, then colonial secretary, indicated his desire for legislature to reform the present state of the coinage. In later correspondence of 1774 Boulton referred to the possibility of harnessing steam power to the coin press. Assisted by friends and petitions Boulton was the principal influence upon the government forming a Committee of the Privy Council to reform the coinage. He appeared before them on January 15th 1788 and by such conviction of views obtained authorisation to strike some pattern halfpenny pieces based upon his own ideas. The work was executed in Paris by a French die-sinker Jean Pierre Droz, there being nobody capable in England to operate the newly invented segmented collars. The pieces were presented to the Council in May. Some bore the edge legend 'Render unto Caeser the things that are Caesers' being struck on a new press at Soho and Boulton further offered to manufacture the new coin at less than half the cost of the old. The patterns were finally approved although much delay ensued due to a reluctance for change at the Royal Mint. Boulton, on the contrary, began immediate preparations for a complete coining plant and although having only recently constructed several presses – with which a hundred tons of coin was struck for the Honourable East India Company – he decided on new equipment engaging steam power for motivation and rehoused all the apparatus in a new building later known as the Soho Mint. By the close of 1788 the premises were complete with automation introduced along production lines where ever possible reducing handling to a minimum. Indeed such an establishment had never been witnessed before and Boulton believed, even if his contemporaries doubted, that this would not only prosper Britain and her growing empire but far more profoundly alter the destiny of the world.

Sampled on the new machinery were two coinages, a silver order for Sierra Leone and one of copper for the American colonies. Boulton not only lobbied members of parliament for reform but also made practical contributions by issuing tokens of correct weight and fineness to raise circulatory standards, one of the better known pieces being struck for his friend John Wilkinson. So satisfied was Boulton with his enterprise he took out letters patent for 'an application of motive power to stamping and coining' which was granted on July 8th 1790 being number 1757. Boulton's machinery by 1798 had a capacity of twelve hundred tons whereupon the market price of copper quickly increased and any previous surplus vanished. Accompanying this copper price rise white button makers lowered their employee's wages, thus offsetting their losses whilst maintaining competitive pricing. Boulton was blamed and so riotous had the button workers become he decided to fortify Soho with armament but by chance justice prevailed.

At an age of almost seventy in the summer of 1797, Boulton undertook his most cherished ambition. His persistence was rewarded by a contract calling for copper coin of the realm. Their prime intention was to cease the blatent counterfeit coppers which engulfed the economy but as these coins held such importance in every-day retail trade, rather than discredit them quicker than they could be replaced, an order for 500 tonnes was tendered twenty tonnes of which would be twopences. These coins were so designed to function as weights and measures and they duly appeared in July 1797 being legal tender to one shilling. Copper began rising in price resulting in the halfpenny and farthing issue being struck fractionally lighter and legal tender to sixpence. By 1805 the Napoleonic wars had raised copper to £165 per tonne and the coinage weight collapsed to twenty-four pence per pound actually lighter than Tower issues of the previous century. These weights catered for further price rises which never materialised but the falling price of copper came a little late to prevent many earlier cart-wheels going into the melting-pot – although twopences had a saving grace being useful as weights for traders. The final issue appeared in 1806 and 1807 their weight not disturbed again until the bronze issue of 1860. Boulton's coppers comprised some 45,407,440 pieces and according to Joseph Sage, a mint official, their weight at sixteen per pound 'only erred 1/2425 too little'. Boulton died ultimately on August 17th 1809 reconciled that his life's work had fostered the economic growth of the world.

If Boulton became coherent and organised the government remained the contrary. Only with constant pressure by this gentleman and others was the Committee of the Privy Council set into motion. So grave was the coinage position that an analysis by the Royal Mint during 1787 revealed three-quarters of the coppers in circulation had never been issued by the mint out of which '8% had some tolerable resemblance to the King's coin, 43% were blatently inferior, 12% were blanks and the balance trash which would disgrace commonsense to suppose it be accepted as coin'. The Committee on coin declared that an increase in weight was more justifiable a remedy than a refinement of workmanship. As most silver coins of earlier issues had been hoarded or exported the main topic for the Committee's discussion was what weight a silver coin should be minted. Conduitt, Master of the Mint, emphasised that gold played a more important role than silver and suggested that 64½ shillings be coined to the pound instead of sixty-two. Amongst the opposition were Locke and Harris who argued gold was too precious to be a standard of value and that the guinea should again be reduced to achieve the same silver and gold ratio as the rest of Europe with worn coin only exchanged as bullion. In a reply the Board of the Mint told the Privy Council that British gold coin had been valued nearly 15¼ times silver since 1717 whilst the French only 14½ and the Dutch 14¾. The Board was inclined to favour the Dutch figure but since the French ratio would bring more dramatic results they suggested a pound of silver represent sixty-five shillings or a reduction in fineness leaving the weight unaltered. Britain had discarded gold in 1797 with the striking of silver coin prohibited any necessary issue being provided by countermarked foreign coins.

Upon the recommendations of Lord Liverpool the Coin Committee resolved in early 1816 that gold should be the only standard in law by abolishing bimetallism and reducing the silver coinage to token status. They suggested the pound troy be coined into sixty-six shillings rather than sixty-two – being neither low enough to encourage melting nor high enough to tempt counterfeiting. The Bill effecting these recommendations fell into severe opposition from both sides of the House by members believing silver to have the only standard of value. The second Lord Liverpool defended the motion with brilliant eloquence and the Bill became enacted on June 22nd 1816. The Committee, however, wished the guinea to remain but public preference for pounds, to which they had become accustomed by paper money, somewhat influenced their decision for pounds. That the gold coinage should be brought back to the unit of twenty shillings was not decided until August 3rd 1816 well after the Act was passed. The values of the coins came down in exact proportions due to the Mint's unaltered price of gold. The new twenty shilling coin soon revived the old name 'sovereign' and although much pricing still continued in guineas, this denomination lapsed into money of account.

A silver coinage without limit was planned but upset by a missing proclamation which would have given private citizens the right to have their own silver coined into money. Because of its omittance the Mint gave preference to the Bank of England which in turn now controlled the silver circulation as well as gold. When silver failed to reach sixty-two shillings it was too tempting to present at the Mint and on any rare occasion it exceeded this amount no coining would ensue. This evaded right for persons to have their own silver minted was abolished in 1870. William Wellesley Pole the second Earl of Mornington and brother of the Duke of Wellington, was appointed Mint Master and his main concern were staffing arrangements at the new Mint.

The aesthetic endeavourments of Pole and the Committee curtailed coinage patterns of a conventional style. For centuries a denomination's design remained loyal from one reign to the next, any alteration only for ease of identification. Although Thomas Wyon and his family along with his cousin William were established at the Mint, Pole agitated for foreign interest and engaged Benedetto Pistrucci being impressed with his ring cameo of St.George and the Dragon. Pistrucci was paid over three hundred pounds to prepare models for the new coinage in jasper with a St.George, modelled from a hotel waiter, executed in wax for a coin reverse. The St. George motif had been adopted by many east European countries from time to time and Pistrucci had made many cameos in Italy of similar style, but he probably drew direct inspiration from a shell cameo the 'Batielle Coquelle' in the Duke of Orleans collection. Few achieved the poise and equilibrium rendered by Pistrucci, who from his earliest childhood had learnt much of horses from stables at his home and was an accomplished horseman. Some critisism was levelled at the design insomuch that when the hero delivered his blow, through lack of counterbalance he would fall from his horse. However, Pistrucci is careful to show St.George's left foot firmly against the horse. For the three portraits executed by him the first was rejected, the second adapted by Wyon for the sixpence and shilling and the third for a halfcrown was suspended upon its appearance to the public. Pistrucci did not appreciate the great forces used in coinage which demanded different contour and relief design from his usual work. He misplaced the blame on Wyon and as a result learnt how to cut steel dies for himself. During 1817 he retouched Wyon's dies made from his effigies and cut the second head for the halfcrown along with a steel matrix for his celebrated St.George. On the sovereign St.George is depicted holding a broken lance but Wyon reworked this die substituting a sword, which although inappropriate gave a more pronounced appearance.

The moment samples of the sixpence and shilling had received the Prince Regent's approval work began immediately. By mid-August rolling rooms were working around the clock with other shops from dawn to dusk and by the year's end nearly two million pounds in coin was ready for distribution. Not only sixpences and shillings but half a million halfcrowns were made well in advance of approval during early 1817. Mint Master Pole gave formal notice of issue and the new silver coins appeared on February 17th 1817. On the first of March all previous silver was demonatised allowing three months grace in which the public could surrender it at face value upon presentation at any of 623 exchange stations opened for its reception. Out of two and a half million pounds of coin received only seven thousand pounds was rejected. The number of counterfeits accepted was very high and much running fifteen to a hundred points below sterling. The average loss of weight was found to be 22½% making a loss to the exchequer of three-quarters of a million pounds. Mere collection entailed fifty thousand pounds expenditure but this was offset by profit on the new coin. Recoinage of the old coin was complete by May 1817 and the gold sovereign was proclaimed legal tender in July. Paradoxically the public preferred paper currency and gold did not pass readily into circulation. These coins were kept mainly as curios and taken abroad by travellers to France. Gold minting declined sharply in 1818 and negligible for the rest of this reign.

The five-shilling piece, although of prime intent for connoisseurs did circulate upon its appearance in late 1818. Endless patience was lavished at each stage of its progress and special collars were designed with the coin struck by several gradual blows. The almost proof-like crowns received final care by despatch within tissued crates and all who handled them warned they were works of art. The design by Pistrucci exemplifies the renewed revivalism that caught the monarchies of Europe for classical portrayal. Both Pistrucci's head of George III and the St.George reverse show art in more academic terms and reflect this radical change from Baroque. The coin design was handled roughly by the press, disparaging the addition of the Mint Master's initials along with Pistrucci's full name. The one point escaping attention was the King's portrait bore no resemblance to the monarch's dishevelled appearance. Coinage of all crown pieces ceased late 1822.

In 1820 the Mint began issuing sixty ounce gold bars for paying redeemable notes for the first time in twenty-three years. A statute for full return to gold was anticipated and cash payments without restriction were resumed in May 1820. With the withdrawal of smaller Bank of England notes output of gold soared to nearly ten million pounds in 1821 besides half a million pounds of silver coin. All these new coins bore Pistrucci's portrait of George IV, the crown being considered the handsomest coin in Europe although struck for only eighteen months. The halfcrown, shilling and sixpence designs were practically identical with the emblems of the kingdom rather inelegantly arranged around the Royal escutcheon. The portrait, employing a rich basic texture of fine relief and in excellent style was, however, too life-like for the King who demanded a change to the more complimentary tone of Sir Francis Chantry's portraiture. Pistrucci refused to simulate another artist whereupon the Mint disengaged his services losing seventeen hundred pounds already advanced for his Waterloo medal, although Pistrucci promised to complete this medal in due course.

The beautiful reverses of both this and the next reign's coinage were engraved by Jean Baptiste Merlen a Frenchman engaged at the request of Pistrucci. With the introduction of the double-sovereign for currency in 1823 Merlen achieved moderate success with his portrait for this coin but these pieces hardly circulated and were not to reappear for over sixty years. During 1826 the principal engravers at the Mint produced around two hundred specimen sets similar to Boulton's and established a precedent for future issues. The coins were struck in proof state with currency pieces augmented by several patterns illustrating all possible denominations of the realm and these sets would have been distributed amongst officials in government circles.

Many improvements were devised in these early years of the Tower Hill mint. Sir John Barton designed a draw bench whereby the end of a silver fillet was inserted into a pair of bevelled steel plates, then dragged through by an endless chain enabling greater accuracy gauging thickness and a sizeable step forward in production. Better coin weight tolerance was achieved and this resulted in the prohibition of filing heavy blanks especially with Pole's cherished crowns. This draw bench technique was finally displaced in 1905 with improved rolling mills. The advent of steam had forced dies to operate under greater pressure and more improved steel alloys were discovered in 1823 by William Brande, professor of chemistry at the Royal Institute.

The Bank of England was the principal customer for the Mint's coinage but had lost the absolute monopoly of the eighteenth century. Provided it was in ingot form any one could tender gold bullion for coining on condition that the amount exceeded ten thousand pounds and at least twenty carats fineness. Articles not in bullion form could only be undertaken provided the customer paid for their refining. Gold received for coinage often contained silver as part of the alloy which the Mint merely added copper to bring to the required carat. Unfortunately a French chemist discovered a profitable process for the separation of minute percentages of any silver in gold or gold within silver and from 1825 vast quantities of sovereigns were exported to Paris, where the small quantity of silver and other sundry metals contained in the sovereigns were recovered. This waste of gold sovereigns, which was cheaper to export than gold bars, had to cease but do so only when methods had been found to remove this silver. Appointed to the Royal Mint as melter was Gilbert Mathieson who by chance had discovered what the process entailed from a discharged employee of a French firm. Mathieson ultimately founded the famous refinery bearing his name in 1829 and as soon as his works were opened he was profitably extracting gold from sixpences which the Bank of England had discarded during that year.

Gold when tendered for coinage also contained small traces of iridium and platinum, often too small to detect in assay but which nevertheless caused cracking during blanking and stamping. Irrespective of how late this occurred in manufacture the gold was always returned to the Bank of England. Finally the Bank protected itself by requiring customers to have certificates showing the gold had been treated at Mathieson's works. A considerable problem during this period was the fixation for the standards of fineness. The standard gold trial plate of 1688 and silver trial plate of 1728 had been virtually used by 1828 and were found to be two thousandth below fineness for gold and rather more than four thousandth too fine for silver. Even the new plates, after repeated verification by the Paris and Amsterdam mints, were found more than one thousandth short due to an unforeseen miscalculation of silver residue. The Mint decided to recover this loss by gradual stages so that suprisingly the full legal weight of a sovereign was not achieved until 1851.

The coinage by 1830 exhibited a variety unmatched to the present-day with over thirty different crowns issued along with over forty better known patterns, struck in half a dozen different metals. Although about nine million pounds of silver coin had been issued up to the accession of William IV, the government anticipated heavy demand for crowns following the prohibition of county banknotes less than five pounds. To buy the necessary bullion a quarter of a million pounds was borrowed from Army funds but the demand, however, did not arise and indeed the banks complained of having too much silver coin. Coupled with their waning popularity this ensured the beautiful pattern crowns of William IV remained unadopted for currency. However, the money was used to coin a stock of sovereigns whereby bullion owners could be paid three-quarters consignment value without delay. This gold coinage fund ran for two years during which nearly four millions were coined, almost all for Messrs. Rothschild the remainder for several large brokers. Because the fund's prime intention was for smaller clients' benefit, the fund was abandonded and the Army rebursed. After this private consignment to the Mint was unusual and expensive, the last occasion in 1871 when a small ingot tendered by a Member of Parliament produced a hundred sovereigns.

The coronation of William IV was commemorated by an issue of about two hundred engravers' proof sets but unlike the preceeding issue the five pound piece was omitted. Certain denominations of these silver proofs including the crown appear struck in a form of white metal, softer than sterling silver and similar to an electrotype, enabling them to be indented with a fingernail. The two pound piece likewise appears struck in Barton's metal but using a lead based flan for achieving the correct weight. The engravers were not obliged to use currency alloy as proof coins are not legal tender therefore further research may clarify their exact composition. The persistence of striking coins in exotic metals continued as with the previous reign. Crowns are found struck in gold, copper and lead with sovereigns in platinum, and sixpences in palladium supplemented by new experimental pieces such as the quarter sovereign. Any apparent lack of originality in William IV coinage is recompensed with a purity of style achieved by both Wyon and Merlen. The shilling and sixpence reverses by Merlen utilise a wreath of oak and olive, a design remaining loyal for eighty years. To avoid confusion between the sixpence and half-sovereign the latter was reduced in diameter by one sixteenth for the 1834 issue, but banks made such protest on behalf of customers that the Mint was obliged to recoin these back to their previous diameter, although forty thousand had been issued at a cost of nine hundred pounds.

With the coinage of the late King terminated upon the accession of Victoria, William Wyon began trial sovereign strikings bearing his portrait of the young Queen. This splendid effigy was the more remarkable for being produced within six weeks and yet employed upon many world currencies for over fifty years. The reverses of the smaller silver coins continued the designs from the previous reign. The crown, halfcrown and sovereign employed a new reverse depicting the Royal shield surrounded by a wreath of olive. The Royal escutcheon was now devoid of the Hanoverian arms, as under Salic law Hanover had now passed to the Duke of Cumberland. The coronation witnessed the third issue of engravers' proof sets. The spade-shaped case contained Wyon's celebrated five pound piece portraying Queen Victoria as 'Una' the heroine of Edmund Spenser's poem

'The Faerie Queen' first published in 1591. 'Una' literally meaning 'the one', is shown guiding the British lion with her sceptre and although medallic in presentation still remains a most beautiful pattern.

Both parliament and the Bank of England were anxious not to see currency conditions of the eighteenth century return and in consequence all coins received attention after issue. Gold was of prime importance for its use as an international currency demanded it be kept in good fettle. With the introduction of the sovereign, the mean tolerance allowed was one half grain and although raised to three-quarters of a grain in 1821 was only half that allowed for the former guinea. The sovereign's life was eighteen years and the half-sovereign's only nine, wearing faster due to a greater proportion of area to mass. So costly was the gold maintenance a motion was tabled that the half-sovereign might become of token value containing nine shillings of gold. A further suggestion was that the Bank of England's profit on notes should off-set gold coinage costs. By 1880 over half the sovereigns in the country were estimated to be threepence light. Other than the Bank of England this loss was disregarded by bankers and general public alike, any one noticing that the critical weight had passed received only bullion value less twopence for presentation and melting charges, hence light gold coin was noticed only by the Bank itself. By 1842 different values had been achieved for full and lightweight sovereigns and a proclamation was voted which as a concession, gold would be received at the full mint rate of £3.17.10½d per ounce relieved of the usual fourpence halfpenny tariff. Under these terms fourteen million pounds of light gold was received for refining and by 1845 a third of all gold currency had been recoined involving expenditure of sixty-five thousand pounds. From here onwards the Mint annually withdrew a half-million pounds in light gold coin although this comparatively large figure was still rather less than the rate of decline.

The Bank was constantly pressuring for worn silver coinage to be withdrawn but the Mint would only consider this coinage at bullion rate and after pressure by the Bank it was agreed that the Mint should pay the issue figure per pound, whilst the Bank bore any loss in weight. Half a million pounds of sixpences and shillings were melted in 1831 with sixpences having lost almost five percentage of weight during their short life. The continuous withdrawal of sixpences and shillings commenced during 1846 entirely at mint expense but halfcrowns were not so withdrawn until 1871 and florins rarely removed at all.

Commerce was still severely handicapped by lack of small denominations. Coppers formed the basic currency for small transactions but being cumbersome in service and costly to maintain a large issue of a Maundy coin seemed the logical decision. Joseph Hume M.P. proposed the groat, later supplimented by the threepence, and in 1836 the small grained edged coin appeared portraying Wyon's 'Britannia'. This coin represented the identical charge for a half-mile hackney cab fare and the drivers, resenting its introduction as there would be no room for tipping, styled the coin 'Joey'. With the introduction of the threepence for domestic service in 1839 harmony was never achieved between these two denominations and the groat was suspended in 1856. Both coins were supplied by the Mint to whomsoever required them, as in the case of coppers, unlike larger denominations which were issued only at the Bank's discretion.

The minting programme was entirely predicted by the Bank. However, in 1840 the Mint realised no stocks of silver were maintained and proposed coining upwards of a quarter of a million pounds against immediate orders it might receive from the Bank, for although amply preoccupied with gold recoinage the silver department remained quiet. The Chancellor resisted the proposal and in consequence no stocks of early Victorian silver were kept. Crowns made an undue appearance during 1844 and although of long-standing unpopularity, gained some interest in 1847 by an introduction of the Wyon-Dyce 'Gothic' design on a series of pattern pieces. Though ill-favoured in England crowns were in use elsewhere as *The Times* commented, 'Yet two thousand pounds of these coins are made and sent to the Falkland Islands. There the whalers, English, German, Swedes and Americans, assemble to pass winter in harbour and the only accepted currency is the English five-shilling piece'.

An attempt was made during the late 1840's to place sterling on a decimal basis. This was nothing new for in 1682 the economist Sir William Petty advocated farthings be made five a penny and later Sir Christopher Wren would have coined an ounce of silver into a hundred parts. The United States had adopted a decimal basis from the Mexican dollar supplimented by English pence whilst the French revolutionists had achieved similar by dividing the sou into five parts, originally forming a twentieth of a franc. Napoleon replaced disorderly European currencies with French denominations. These events stirred continual support for decimalisation of sterling and two commissions of 1841 and 1843 reported favourably towards decimal coinage. Sir John Bowring won considerable support in the House of Commons for his motion supporting decimalisation, upon which the Government promised the immediate introduction of a coin equalling a tenth of a pound. This coin duly appeared in 1849 stemming from a multitude of patterns the previous year, with suggestions for its name including dime, decade and centum, to the adopted title 'florin' designated from a Dutch silver coin then current in Holland. The obverse interpreted the Gothic revivalism by an almost direct adaptation of Wyon's earlier portrait from his crown of 1847. Dyce's reverse stressed its objective with the legend, 'one tenth of a pound', whilst the obverse carried the simple inscription, 'Victoria Regina 1849' at the suggestion of the Prince Consort. The use of a single title not unknown particularly with coins of British India where 'Victoria Queen' and 'Victoria Empress' were used. However, the British public were overwrought by the omission of 'dei gratia' and 'fid def' and expected these presumptions from this 'Godless and Graceless' florin.

Political intrigue soon developed hastened because Mint Master Shiel was of Irish extraction and as a Roman Catholic suspected of engineering a plot to overthrow the Protestant government. After an issue of nearly half a million pieces, Shiel apologised in Parliament and the usual titles appeared with subsequent issues. To give the florin sufficent grounding half-crowns were temporarily discontinued but re-established from results of a circular letter addressed to the bankers of London in 1874. Thomas Graham F.R.S., Professor of Chemistry at University College, London, was appointed Master in 1856 and his interest in metallurgy again prompted striking currency pieces in various metals, and establishing their reaction to gases. His main contribution to English numismatics was instituting a standardization for dating British coin, whereby the date on a coin represents that year it comes from the presses. Formerly if the coming year's coinage was predicted of short issue, that coinage was often struck from the previous year's dies. This practice accounts for any variance between a given mintage figure with perhaps a contradicting rarity. Although this system was rigidly enforced in 1864 for British coinage some colonies continued with the old policy, and a few even preferring one type of coinage bearing a single date. Coinciding with this date change policy during 1864, privy numbers were placed on gold and silver coinage for registration purposes, each die number applicable to a certain employee with the largest minting years having the highest series of numbers. The ancient 'Trial of the Pyx' remained unaltered, with two pieces of silver set aside for examination from each 'journey weight' or seven hundred and twenty ounces of silver, originally derived from the Norman word 'journee' meaning 'a day's work'. One piece was examined by the Mint Assayer before issuing the 'journey', whilst the other retained for the jury of the Goldsmiths' Company elected for the annual Trial of the Pyx. A significant change during Graham's mastership was the replacement of heavy copper pennies by a lighter bronze issue.

In the summer of 1887 the Queen celebrated her Golden Jubilee on the British throne and in commemoration the gold and silver coinage was remodelled. Considering the ample time there had been for preparation the Jubilee coinage, whilst superbly executed, did have some disappointments with design. The new portrait was sought by competition amongst eminent artists, the least unsuccessful being an effigy by Joseph Edgar Boehm R.A. an Austro-Hungarian, whilst the reverses were readaptations of Georgian issues. The monarch was depicted wearing a miniature crown purchased for domestic use to escape full regalia. By reviving similar reverses for the half-sovereign and sixpence the latter was frequently gilded, causing the discarded 'wreath' design to be immediately reintroduced. The shilling's portrait was of such insignificant size that the whole head was enlarged in

1889. The first introduction of the double-florin since 1619 was intended to compliment the florin for decimalisation but its unprecedented appearance and close resemblance to the crown only allowed a mintage for four years, being discontinued in 1890. These coins, euphemistically termed 'radiating tea trays and pokers', were so unsuccessful that never before in the Mint's history had a denomination been issued whilst simultaneously received back as bullion. Criticism of the new currency persuaded a Committee to be established for procuring new designs and in 1892 the Committee favoured a new portrait by Thomas Brock, with reverses modelled by Edward Poynter R.A., the celebrated painter and these designs continued until the end of Victoria's reign.

George William DeSaulles, the first salaried engraver, designed a pantographically produced series of Edward VII portraits for the entire range of denominations. Only the legend arrangement varied which now included 'Britanniarum Omnium', added in recognition for the Empire's assistance during the Boer War. The coronation produced the customary issue of proof sets in octagonal cases, standardized for the first time, but with the traditional brilliant field rendered matt by treatment with acid. Although a short and uneventful issue, due to contemporary neglect this series has become very scarce in mint state, notably with the earlier years. During 1904 the Mint sustained its first productive loss for whilst silver was at its lowest price for centuries, there was little call for any coinage. The demands of Prussia after her victory with France, coupled with the widespread adoption of gold monometallism, caused silver to gradually depreciate by having less affinity with gold. The Latin Union was virtually forced to coin silver on demand and between 1890 and 1915 the value of silver had halved.

The last complete gold and silver coinage struck for circulation carried an effigy of George V by Sir Bertram Mackennal with reverses adopted or modified from previous reigns. The mintages prior to the Great War follow closely those of Edward VII and as scarce to obtain in perfect condition. During late 1914 in consequence of the war, minting considerably increased and although the price of silver was rising a large profit accrued because of unprecedented output. Steel shortages were forcing dies into longer service and well-struck mint specimens from initially sharp relief dies are very scarce. The London Commodity Exchange recorded silver at its highest ever price on February 11th 1920, producing a premium of over one third legal-tender value. Rather than suspend minting temporarily and allow silver to stabilize, a Bill became hastily enacted requiring British silver coinage be reduced to half fineness, despite many Empire currencies continuing almost undisturbed and silver itself lowering in price.

With no preparation having been granted for debasement there was little concept how the new fineness would react under minting conditions. The initial alloy of half silver and half copper was superseded by one using discarded cupro-nickel bullet envelopes producing a ten percent nickel content. This not only resulted in greater fuel costs for the Mint due to a higher melting point, but by not being a true alloy the fineness varied within each ingot. In consequence discolouration not only occurred but rolling and stamping caused considerable 'lapping' with portions of the surface flaking easily from slight circulation. In late 1921 the nickel content was replaced by five percent manganese but this fleeting issue quickly 'coppered'. During 1922 the original concept of half copper and half silver was revived with flans deeply blanched inducing a higher percentage of silver on coin surfaces. The final adjustment for the last issue of George V included five percent nickel and five percent zinc in its composition which proved the most satisfactory.

During 1921 experiments were undertaken with all silver standards used by various governments ranging from the adopted .500 fineness through to .900 fineness with .720 fineness proving the ideal composition, which was introduced into the Netherlands that year. Shillings were chosen to be struck in these trial alloys and again in pure nickel during 1923 and 1924 when an abandonment of silver seemed possible. Kruger Gray produced a small series of nickel patterns when this change in metal became envisaged, selecting oak-leaves and acorns for the threepence and sixpence reverse motifs and restyling the Royal cypher on the shilling, with all coins having a remodelled portrait or 'modified effigy'. These designs were later used on the continuing silver issues, obverses during 1926 and reverses the following year, with a silver proof set to confirm these new coins. A crown piece was included, the first for over twenty-five years, instigated at the suggestion of Sir Charles Oman then President of the Royal Numismatic Society.

Towards the close of his reign George V celebrated his silver Jubilee by the issue of a commemorative crown. Although adopting the definitive portrait the legend stops and spacing were incorrectly arranged, whilst the reverse employed Percy Metcalfe's art deco St.George, a remarkable contrast from previous issues.

Gold coinage only occurred the first few years of this reign, when the gold standard effectively collapsed having encountered the outbreak of World War, its first obstacle in almost fifty years. Any import or export of gold, the very tenet of a gold standard, proved undesirable and difficult partly through a 'U' boat blockade, and the gold standard was officially abandoned in 1919 with any export prohibited. However, Winston Churchill revived the concept in 1925 with an ability to redeem banknotes for four hundred ounce 'good delivery' bars at pre-war values being Sir Isaac Newton's original 1717 price of £4 4s 11½d per ounce. This measure attempted to reduce the value of gold by nearly one third its post-war 'free' level and this policy survived only six years.

No coins bearing the portrait and titles of Edward VIII were issued for Great Britain although coins dated 1936 for George V were struck during this reign. Specimen gold and silver sets without half-sovereign are known with the King's portrait, at his own wish and against precedence, positioned facing left. After the abdication some Edward reverse dies were utilised for the currency coinage of George VI, including the 'Scottish' shilling depicting a lion *sejant*. This was accompanied by another showing the 'English' Royal cypher and both types were issued until the end of the sterling series. Ironically Kruger Gray devised a suspended 'peace' shield reverse for the halfcrown, replacing the 'war' shield with lance opening from the previous reign. Gold and silver proof sets were struck for the coronation in 1937 with the four gold coins being separately cased. Silver threepences were finally replaced by 1945 with a dodecagonal nickel-brass coin, both concurrently issued since 1937.

The substitution of a base-metal for silver issues originally considered in the early twenties, ultimately came in 1947 almost paralleling circumstances of the first debasement. For during and two years after both World Wars over five thousand tonnes of fine silver was minted, only to be recoined following each debasement. Although the intrinsic content rarely exceeded face value until recently, the Mint itself could be profitably engaged merely replacing the old silver coins with new cupro-nickel. Electronic machinery was installed to assist retrieving these silver coins from circulation, which in turn defrayed the Lend-lease debt finally repaid in 1957. From 1947 Maundy coins were returned to sterling silver standard. India having gained independence in 1947 necessitated the removal of 'Indiae Imperator' from coinage titles and these were relinquished after 1948, with the sixpence remodelled from an Imperial to a Royal cypher. A mid-century proof set was issued in 1950 with another the following year for the National Exhibition. This set contained the first base-metal crown commemorating both the festival and the denomination's quatercentenary.

The coinage of Her Majesty, after the coronation year, required further modification due to the changing status of overseas possessions. 'Omnium' and for some reason 'Britanniar' were therefore considered inappropriate and subsequently omitted. Cupro-nickel proof sets were issued for the coronation with gold proof sets, struck to maintain the series, remaining in official custody. An effigy by Mary Gillick was employed on all duo-decimal issues and had an unbroken legend, last employed some three hundred years ago. The Caroline equestrian design for the crown of 1953 depicts Her Majesty seated on the Police horse 'Winston', with the reverse showing a Welsh leek accompanying the national emblems for the first time. Two further crowns were issued for the sterling series. The 1960 crown was primarily for the British Trade Exposition held in New York with the Royal Mint in attendance striking commemorative medals. Also issued was a special polished die crown struck in London, as overseas striking of British coinage is forbidden, with an ordinary issue available from general banks. The last sterling crown appeared in 1965 commemorating the passing of Sir Winston Churchill, only the second portrayal of a commoner since the conquest, with Sir Winston wearing the famous siren-suit from his war time leadership modelled by Oscar Nemon. Gold sovereigns resumed production during 1957 for external use and this also consolidated their legal tender status. This was the first resumption since 1925, although restrikings with slightly firmer edges, were struck with this date after the war.

The well-designed minor coinage of this reign continued themes from previous issues, with both shillings again representing the two kingdoms. A Committee of Enquiry was established in late 1961 under Earl Halsbury, and proposed coining the pound sterling into one hundred pence, retaining the florin, shilling and sixpence. To discourage unwanted speculation and simplify production for the final sterling issues, all pieces coined from 1967 were struck with this date. Decimalisation became implimented on the 15th of February 1971 with the transfer of production to Llantrisant bringing to a conclusion the English silver coins of Tower Hill.

ABBREVIATIONS

Coron	Coronetted	Obv	Obverse
Cu.Ni	Copper nickel	Rev	Reverse
Des	Designer	RH	Right hand
Hd	Head	Sov	Sovereign
Laur	Laureated	YH	Young head
LH	Left hand	'*'	to be confirmed

NOTES

All coins are milled edge unless stated.
All prices are for mint state specimens.
All lettered-edged crowns are 'Decus et Tutamen Anno Regni' with Latin or Roman numerals unless stated.
All weights are troy ounces of 480 grains.
All die-axes from the Jubilee coinage onwards are '↑↑' i.e. both 'upright'.

NUMBERING

All currency pieces are numbered in the left-hand margin.
Special strikings are differentiated by adding their column heading letters to these left-hand numbers.
Thus an 1874 currency halfcrown is (B.S.C.) 579, whilst in gold (B.S.C.) 579G.
Single line entries need not adopt any lettering.

Duodecimal Issues

of

Tower Hill

1816 - 1970

GEORGE III

24th May 1738 – 29th January 1820

CROWNS

Des: B.Pistrucci

Obverse 1

Dies ↑↓

Des: B.Pistrucci

Reverse A

No.	Dies		Raised EDGE YEAR	DATE	MINT STATE	P PROOF	E PROOF PLAIN EDGE
1	**1 A**		**LVIII**	**1818**	300.00	700.00	
2	–	Incuse edge	–	–		£5800	
3	–	Error edge [1]	–	–	£2200		
4	–		**LIX**	–	310.00		
5	–		–	**1819**	270.00		
6	–	No edge stops	–	–	440.00		
7		'9' over '8'			480.00		
8	–	Thick garter	–	–	530.00		
9	–		**LX**	–	295.00	850.00	£3200
10	–	No stop at 'Tutamen'	–	–	365.00		
11	–		–	**1820**	275.00	950.00	
12	–	'20' over '19'	–	–	550.00		
13	–	'S' of 'Soit' over 'T'	–	–	600.00		

1: Reads: 'Decus Anno Regni et Tutamen. LVIII.'
Note: All edges are read with obv. uppermost. Initials 'W.W.P.' on garter buckle.

Patterns Dated 1817

No.	Designer	OBV.	REV.	P PROOF	E PROOF PLAIN EDGE	G GOLD PLAIN EDGE	C Copper PLAIN EDGE	W WHITE METAL P.Edge
20	W.Wyon	Laur. head,	'Three Graces'		£3300	£24000	£1400	£1700
21	–	– no 'F:D:'	– in lead [2]		650.00			
22	–	– tiny thistle	– – [2]		500.00			
23	–	Laur. draped bust,	'Incorrupta'		£5500	£28000		
24	Pistrucci [1]	'Britanniarum', no border beads [2]			£7800			
25	–	–	,with –	£6000		*		
26	–	'Britanniar' [3]	'St. George'	£7700				

1: All Pistrucci patterns have laur. head & St. George reverses.
2: On a thick flan.
3: Edge year 'Quinquagesimo Ꝝ septimo' incuse – coin has matt finish.
All other edged Pistrucci patterns are dated 'LVIII' etc. in raised letters except no.s 33, 34L & 37 which are incuse – no. 30 remains uncertain.

Patterns Dated 1818

No.	Designer	OBV.	REV.	P PROOF	E PROOF PLAIN EDGE	G GOLD PLAIN EDGE	W WHITE METAL P.Edge	L LEAD PLAIN EDGE
30	Pistrucci	Large laur. head,	with pellet [1]	£6200				750.00
31	—	— wide flan	—					800.00
32	—	—	no pellet	£6200	£6000	£32000	£2000	
33	—	— small edge letters	— [2]	£6700				
34	—	—	large rev. beads	£7000 [3]				800.00
35	—	—	no —		£6800 [3]			
36	—	Laur. head 'DG' close, rose stops		£5000				
37	—	— —	star —	£5800				
38	—	— —			£6000			
39	—	As currency – short laurel ties,					£1800	

1: This pellet below St. George's thigh, assisted Pistrucci to centralise the puncheon, locating dead centre of the finished die. All Pistrucci patterns have 'St. George' rev.
2: May also exist with incuse edge. 3: Struck from unpolished dies.

HALFCROWNS

Des: B.Pistrucci

Des: T.Wyon

Obverse 1 *Dies* ↑↑ Reverse A

No.	Dies	DATE	MINT STATE	P PROOF	E PROOF PLAIN EDGE	C Copper PROOF
50	**1 A** [1]	**1816**	125.00	580.00	610.00	
51	—	**1817**	130.00	590.00	600.00	480.00

1: 'WWP' incuse left side of shield, 'W' on right side, for W.W.Pole & T.Wyon.

Des: B.Pistrucci

Des: B.Pistrucci

Obverse 1 *Dies* ↑↑ Reverse type

Rev. A
Cross on crown to bead.

Rev. B
Cross on crown to space.

No.	Dies		DATE	MINT STATE	P PROOF	E PROOF PLAIN EDGE
60	**1 A**[1]		**1817**	130.00	570.00	500.00
61	–		**1818**	155.00	650.00	
62	–		**1819**	150.00	610.00	
63	–	'9' over '8'	–	290.00		
64	**1 B**		**1820**	175.00	750.00	660.00

1: 'WWP' on buckle, no 'W' owing to Wyon's death. Rev. B illustration is simulated.

Pattern

No.	Designer	OBV.	REV.	DATE	P PROOF
65	T.Wyon	Laureated small head	Garnished shield	**1817**	£1400

SHILLINGS

Des: Pistrucci Des: T.Wyon

Obverse 1 *Dies* ↑↑ Reverse A

No.	Dies		DATE	MINT STATE	P PROOF	E PROOF PLAIN EDGE	G GOLD PROOF
80	**1 A**[1]		**1816**	24.00	240.00	270.00	£6000
81	–		**1817**	27.00		220.00	
82	–	'R' over 'E' in 'Geor:'	–	300.00			
83	–	'7' higher in date	–	80.00			
84	–		**1818**	125.00			
85	–	'8' higher in date	–	150.00			
86	–		**1819**	35.00			
87	–	'9' over '6'[2]	–	170.00			
88	–	'9' over '8'	–	50.00			
89	–	'9' over '9'[3]	–	70.00			
90	–		**1820**	37.00	250.00		
91	–	'I' over 'S' in 'Honi'	–	160.00			
92	–	'20' over '19'	–	*			
93	–	'20' over '20'	–	110.00			

1: 'WWP' incuse left side of shield, 'W' on right side – for W.W.Pole & T.Wyon.
2: The whole date is faintly double-struck.
3: '9' is either larger or out of alignment on ordinary shillings of 1819.

Pattern

No.	Designer	OBV.	REV.	DATE	P PROOF
94	W.Wyon	Laureated small head	Square garnished shield	undated	£1800

SIXPENCES

Des: Pistrucci Des: T.Wyon

Obverse 1 *Dies* ↑↑ Reverse A

No.	Dies		DATE	MINT STATE	P PROOF	E PROOF PLAIN EDGE	G GOLD PROOF
100	**1 A**[1]		**1816**	22.00			£3500
101	–		**1817**	28.00	270.00	210.00	
102	–		**1818**	36.00	220.00		
103	–		**1819**	35.00	180.00		
104	–	'9' over '8'	–	70.00	170.00		
105	–	small '8'	–	60.00			
106	–		**1820**	52.00	190.00		
107	–	'1' of date inverted	–	170.00			
108	–	'I' over 'S' in 'Honi'	–	180.00			
109	–	small '8'	–	70.00			

1: 'WWP' incuse left side of shield, 'W' on right side, for W.W.Pole & T.Wyon.

Patterns

No.	Designer	OBV.	REV.	DATE	P PROOF	E PROOF PLAIN EDGE	G GOLD PROOF	GG GOLD PLAIN EDGE
110	T.Wyon	Laur. head,	Garter with date	**1816**	950.00	900.00		£3100
111	–	–	Crowned emblems	–			£1750	
112	–	–	–	**1820**				£1900

MAUNDY SETS

Des: Pistrucci Des: W.Wyon

Obverse 1 Reverse A

No.	Dies[1]		DATE	MINT STATE
120	**1 A**	Set of 4d, 3d, 2d & 1d	**1817**	105.00
121	–	–	**1818**	100.00
122	–	–	**1820**	100.00

1: These coins have proof-like surfaces & are plain edged.

GEORGE IV

12th August 1762 – 26th June 1830

CROWNS

Des: B.Pistrucci

Obverse 1

Des: B.Pistrucci

Dies ↑↓

Reverse A

No.	Dies		Raised EDGE YEAR	DATE	MINT STATE	P PROOF	E PROOF PLAIN EDGE	C Copper PROOF	W WHITE METAL P.Edge	L LEAD PLAIN EDGE
130	**1 A**			**1820**			£12500[1]			£1500[1]
131	–		Secundo	**1821**	500.00	£1100[2]		£2000[3]		
132	–		Tertio	–		£3000				
133	–	‘dMM’[4]	Secundo	–	700.00					
134	–		–	**1822**	£1300	£2500				
135	–		Tertio	–	720.00	£1600				
136	–			**1823**			£10500		£3100	

1: This piece has hair streamer & pellet below thigh. 2: Known matt finish (& 131P,471P).
3: Also known with edge year removed & entire edge lettering removed.
4: Initials beneath broken lance are inverted. Note: Edges are read with rev. uppermost.

Des: William Wyon

Obverse 1

Des: Jean B.Merlen

Dies ↑↓

Reverse A

No.	Dies	EDGE YEAR	DATE	P PROOF	E PROOF PLAIN EDGE	C Copper PROOF	B Barton METAL[1] P.Edge
150	**1 A**		**1825**		£4300		£3850
151	–	Septimo	**1826**	£2650[2]	£4000		
152	–	**LVIII**	–	£4600[3]			
153	–	(Octavo)	none			£1650[4]	

1: A thin layer of gold fused to a copper flan. 2: Raised edge. 3: Incuse edge (from previous reign). 4: Incomplete raised edge – ‘Decus et Tutamen’ or ‘et Tutamen Anno Regni’. Another reads ‘Octavo’ but defaced. Date not struck-up & small unfinished head.

Other Patterns

No.	Designer	OBV.	REV.	Raised EDGE YEAR	DATE	P PROOF	E PROOF PLAIN EDGE	C Copper PROOF
160	W.Wyon	Large bare head,	Shield & motto	Septimo	**1828**			£2650[1]
161	–	–	–	Octavo	–			£2750[2]
162	–	–	–	Nono	–	£3800[3]		
163	–	–	–	–	**1829**	£10000		
164	–	–	Shield on mantle	–	–	£9300	£9300	£2500
165	Pistrucci	As currency,	–	–	none			£3250[4]

1: Struck with edge collar from the 1826 issue.
2: This & the 'septimo' edged coin are 'mules' – obv. bears all titles & paired with a rev. of convenience from the previous issue (duplicating legend).
3: Inadvertently sheared as counterfeit.
4: This coin is a mule, with the obv. of convenience duplicating the rev. legend.

HALFCROWNS

Des: B.Pistrucci

Obverse 1

Des: J.B.Merlen

Dies ↑↓ Reverse type

Rev. A Left leg of 'A' to denticle.

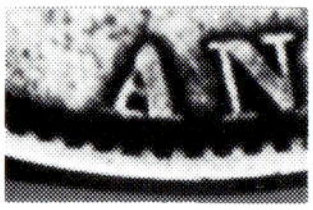

Rev. B Left leg of 'A' to space.

No.	Dies	DATE	MINT STATE	P PROOF	E PROOF PLAIN EDGE
170	**1 A**	**1820**	145.00	510.00	770.00
171	–	**1821**	170.00	600.00	
172	**1 B**[1]		225.00	850.00	
173	–	**1823**	£1700	£2500	
174	–	**1824**		£3250	

1: This reverse has heavier garnishing.

Pattern

No.	Designer	OBV.	REV.	DATE	P PROOF
175	Pistrucci	Laur. head – no initials	As currency	**1820**	850.00

Note: 'J.B.M.' initials are found between rev. border denticles on halfcrowns, or rev. beads on shillings & sixpences, with 'W.W.P.' in shamrock leaves. This applies to coins with 'Pistrucci' obverses. Rev. 'B' illustration is simulated.

Des: Pistrucci

Obverse 1

Dies ↑↓

Des: J.Merlen

Reverse A

No.	Dies	DATE	MINT STATE	P PROOF	E PROOF PLAIN EDGE	C Copper PLAIN EDGE
180	**1 A**	**1822**		£4500[1]	£4300[1]	
181	–	**1823**	180.00	610.00		
182	–	**1824**	240.00	780.00		320.00
183	–	**1825**		*		

1: These coins have beaded garter borders.
*: to be confirmed.

Des: W.Wyon

Obverse 1

Dies ↑↓

Des: J.Merlen

Reverse A

No.	Dies	DATE	MINT STATE	P PROOF	E PROOF PLAIN EDGE	G GOLD PLAIN EDGE	C Copper PLAIN EDGE	B Barton METAL[1] P.Edge
190	**1 A**	**1824**	£3200	£2200	£2500	£9200	580.00	
191	–	**1825**	185.00	580.00	580.00			650.00
192	–	**1826**	165.00	450.00				
193	–	**1828**	300.00					
194	–	**1829**	265.00					

1: A thin layer of gold fused to a copper flan.

Pattern

No.	Designer	OBV.	REV.	DATE	P PROOF
195	**W.Wyon**	Bare head – toothed border,	Shield, – wide flan[1]	**1824**	£2500

1: Irregular flan with oblique 'milling' & indented letter bases, imitating Tower issues. Rev. has heavier garnishing.

SHILLINGS

Des: Pistrucci — Des: J.Merlen

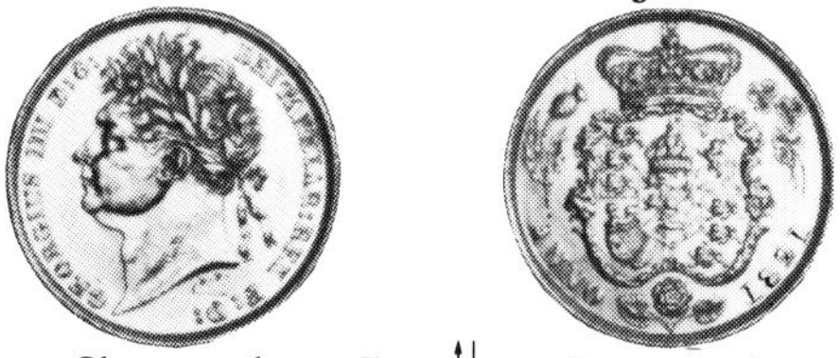

Obverse 1 *Dies* ↑↓ Reverse A

No.	Dies		DATE	MINT STATE	P PROOF
210	**1 A**		**1820**		925.00
211	–		**1821**	125.00	290.00

Des: Pistrucci — Des: J.Merlen

Obverse 1 *Dies* ↑↓ Reverse A

No.	Dies		DATE	MINT STATE	P PROOF
220	**1 A**		**1823**	195.00	400.00
221	–		**1824**	88.00	480.00
222	–		**1825**	82.00	390.00
223	–	'5' over '3'	–	210.00	

Des: W.Wyon — Des: J.Merlen

Obverse type *Dies* ↑↓ Reverse A

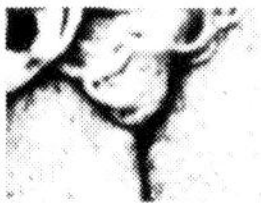

Obv. 1
Less hair to nape of neck.

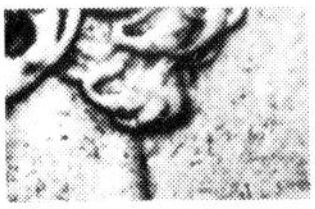

Obv. 2
More hair to nape of neck.

No.	Dies		DATE	MINT STATE	P PROOF	B Barton METAL P.Edge
230	**1 A**		**1825**	55.00	215.00	480.00
231	**2 A**		–	*		
232	–		**1826**	35.00	115.00	
233	–	'6' over '2'	–	200.00		
234	–		**1827**	155.00		
235	–		**1829**	115.00	400.00	

Patterns

No.	Designer	OBV.	REV.	DATE	P PROOF	E PROOF PLAIN EDGE	B Barton METAL[1]
240	W.Wyon	Bare head,	Shield & scroll	**1824**	780.00	670.00	
241	–	–	As 'A' reads: 'Fid: Def:'	**1825**	620.00		540.00

1: A thin layer of gold fused to a copper flan.

SIXPENCES

Des: Pistrucci

Obverse 1

Dies ↑↓

Des: J.Merlen

Reverse A

No.	Dies	DATE	MINT STATE	P PROOF
250	**1 A**	**1820**		930.00
251	–	**1821**	65.00	270.00
252	– reads: 'Bbitanniar'	–	370.00	

Des: Pistrucci

Obverse 1

Dies ↑↓

Des: J.Merlen

Reverse A

No.	Dies	DATE	MINT STATE	P PROOF
260	**1 A**[1]	**1824**	77.00	290.00
261	–	**1825**	57.00	320.00
262	–	**1826**	195.00	400.00

1: These obv. dies are identical to those used for striking half-sovereigns.

Pattern

No.	Designer	OBV.	REV.	DATE	P PROOF
263	Pistrucci	Laureated small head,	As currency	**1826**	650.00

Des: W.Wyon

Des: J.Merlen

Obverse type *Dies* ↑↓ Reverse A

Obv. 1
Double tuft.
'r' of 'Gratia' to space.

Obv. 2
Single tuft.
'r' of 'Gratia' to bead.

No.	Dies	DATE	MINT STATE	P PROOF	R Pewter THICK FLAN
270	**1 A**	**1826**	53.00	*	280.00
271	**2 A**[1]	—	*	120.00	
272	—	**1827**	195.00		
273	—	**1828**	125.00		
274	**1 A**	—	*		
275	—	**1829**	120.00	350.00	

1: Obv. 2 is identical to those dies used for striking currency half-sovereigns.

Pattern

No.	Designer	OBV.	REV.	DATE	P PROOF
276	W.Wyon	Bare head,	As 'A' reads: 'Fid: Def:'	**1825**	680.00

MAUNDY SETS

Des: Pistrucci

Obverse 1

Des: J.Merlen

Reverse A

No.	Dies		DATE	MINT STATE	E PROOF PLAIN EDGE
280	**1 A**[1]	Set of 4d, 3d, 2d & 1d	**1822**	85.00	230.00
281	—	—	**1823**	80.00	
282	—	—	**1824**	110.00	
283	— [2]	—	**1825**	80.00	
284	— [2]	—	**1826**	80.00	
285	—	—	**1827**	80.00	
286		—	**1828**	80.00	270.00
287	—	—	**1829**	80.00	
288	—	—	**1830**	80.00	

1: These coins have proof-like surfaces & are plain edged. The 1822 3d. has small head.
2: 'B' over 'T' known on the 2d. of this year.

WILLIAM IV

21st August 1765 – 20th June 1837

CROWNS

Des: William Wyon — Des: Jean B.Merlen

Obverse 1 — *Dies* ↑↓ — Reverse A

No.	Dies			EDGE YEAR	DATE	P PROOF	E PROOF PLAIN EDGE	G GOLD PLAIN EDGE	L LEAD Raised EDGE
300	**1 A**	'W.W.'	on truncation		**1831**		£4750 [1]	£26000 [2]	
301	–	'W.Wyon'	–	**(LVIII)**	–	*	£5500		
302	–			Tertio	**1832**				£2300
303	–			Septimo	**1834**	£4700 [3]	£7250		

1: Not sterling silver. 2: Weighs 1.285 oz. 3: Incuse: 'Quinquagesimo septimo' & cut.

Other Patterns

No.	Designer	OBV.	REV.	DATE	P PROOF PLAIN EDGE	L LEAD PLAIN EDGE
310	W.Wyon	Bare head,	Shield on mantle with legend	none	£5750	£1400
311	–	–	– smaller garter	–	£8500	

HALFCROWNS

Des: W.Wyon — Des: J.Merlen

Obverse 1 — *Dies* ↑↓ — Reverse A

No.	Dies		DATE	MINT STATE	P PROOF	E PROOF PLAIN EDGE
320	**1 A**	'W.W.' *small obv. beads*	**1831**	£2400		510.00
321	–	*'W.W.' in script*	–		620.00	670.00
322	–	'W.W.'	**1834**	300.00	650.00	
323	–	*'W.W.' in script*	–	180.00	560.00	725.00
324	–		**1835**	270.00		
325	–		**1836**	160.00		725.00
326	–	'6' over '5'	–	270.00		
327	–		**1837**	245.00		

SHILLINGS

Des: W.Wyon Des: J.Merlen

Obverse 1 *Dies* ↑↓ Reverse A

No.	Dies		DATE	MINT STATE	P PROOF	E PROOF PLAIN EDGE	C Copper PLAIN EDGE
340	**1 A**[1]		**1831**		420.00	195.00	
341	–		**1834**	82.00	310.00		
342	–	'3' with round top	–		350.00		
343	–		**1835**	90.00			
344	–	'3' with round top	–		480.00		
345	–		**1836**	80.00			270.00
346	–	'3' with round top	–		480.00		*
347	–		**1837**	115.00	450.00		

1: Pieces dated 1830 were probably struck.

SIXPENCES

Des: W.Wyon Des: J.Merlen

Obverse 1 *Dies* ↑↓ Reverse type

Rev. A
Small design
away from beads.
Thin stems.

Rev. B
Large design
close to beads.
Thick stems.

No.	Dies		DATE	MINT STATE	P PROOF	E PROOF PLAIN EDGE	D PALL-ADIUM P.Edge
360	**1 A**		**1831**	60.00	160.00	90.00	£1800
361	–		**1834**	57.00	195.00		
362	–	'3' with round top	–		240.00		
363	–		**1835**	68.00			
364	–	'3' with round top	–		480.00		
365	–		**1836**	125.00			
366	–	'3' with round top	–		480.00		
367	**1 B**		–	145.00			
368	–		**1837**	90.00	510.00		

Note: Date configurations vary.

GROATS

Des: Wyon | Des: Wyon

Obv. type *Dies*↑↑ Reverse A

Obv. 1
Small head. Low hair. Right legs of 'N's to beads.

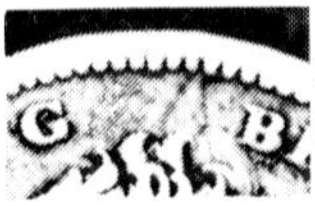

Obv. 2
Large head. High hair. Right legs of 'N's to spaces.

No.	Dies		DATE	MINT STATE	P PROOF	E PROOF PLAIN EDGE	G GOLD PLAIN EDGE
380	**1 A**	reads: 'D: G:'	**1836**	15.00	180.00	120.00	930.00
381	–	thin flan	–				800.00
382	–	reads: 'D : G:'	–	33.00			
383	–		**1837**	45.00	*		
384	**2 A**		–	23.00	300.00		

Patterns

No.	Des.	OBV.	REV.	DATE	P PROOF	E PROOF PLAIN EDGE	G GOLD PLAIN EDGE
390	W.Wyon	Bare head,	'Four pence' over Britannia	**1836**	290.00	330.00	
391	–	–	Large '4' & 'P'	–	250.00	260.00	825.00

THREEPENCES

Des: Wyon | Des: Merlen

Obv. type *Dies*↑↓ Reverse A

Obv. 1
Small head. Low hair. Right legs of 'N's to beads.

Obv. 2
Large head. High hair. Right legs of 'N's to spaces.

No.	Dies[1]	DATE	MINT STATE
400	**1 A**	**1834**	53.00
401	**2 A**	–	40.00
402	**1 A**	**1835**	36.00
403	**2 A**	–	40.00
404	**1 A**	**1836**	38.00
405	**2 A**	–	26.00
406	**1 A**	**1837**	50.00
407	**2 A**	–	*

1: These coins are plain edged.

THREEHALFPENCES

Des: Wyon   Des: Merlen

Obv. 1 *Dies* ↑↓ Rev. A

No.	Dies[1]		DATE	MINT STATE
410	**1 A**		**1834**	22.00
411	–		**1835**	24.00
412	–	'5' over '4'	–	50.00
413	–		**1836**	27.00
414	–		**1837**	65.00

1: Although of Imperial type, these coins were issued for colonial use – primarily for the West Indies after emancipation. They are plain edged.

MAUNDY SETS

Des: W.Wyon   Des: J.Merlen

Obverse 1   Reverse A

No.	Dies[1]		DATE	MINT STATE	E PROOF PLAIN EDGE	G GOLD PLAIN EDGE	3d Dies[2]
420	**1 A**	Set of 4d, 3d, 2d & 1d	**1831**	90.00	150.00	£4700	1 A
421	–	–	**1832**	80.00			–
422	–	–	**1833**	80.00			–
423	–	–	**1834**	80.00			2 A
424	–	–	**1835**	80.00			
425	–	–	**1836**	80.00			
426	–	–	**1837**	80.00			

1: These coins have proof-like surfaces & are plain edged.
2: These dies, where noted, are from the threepence series.

VICTORIA

24th May 1819 – 22nd January 1901

CROWNS

Des: William Wyon — Des: Jean B. Merlen

Obverse 1 — *Dies* ↑↓ — Reverse A

No.	Dies		Incuse EDGE YEAR	DATE	MINT STATE	P PROOF	E PROOF PLAIN EDGE
430	**1 A**			**1839**			£2600 [1]
431	–	Edge stops 'stars'	**VIII**	**1844**	£2200		
432	–	– 'cinquefoils'	–	–	£2100	£3400	
433	–	– –	–	**1845**	£2000	£3600	
434	–	Large date	–	–	£2200		
435	–	–	**XI**	**1847**	£3000		
436	–		milled	–	£6700		
437	–			**1879**			£15000

Note: Edges read with either obv. or rev. uppermost.

Patterns

No.	Des.	OBV.	REV.	EDGE YEAR	DATE	P PROOF	E PROOF PLAIN EDGE	G GOLD PLAIN EDGE
450	W.Wyon	Y.H. as currency,[1]	'Una & lion'[2]	Tertio	**1839**	£7500[3]	£8300	£30000
451	–	– 'Britanniarum'[4]	–	–	–	£8000		£21000[5]
452	–	– –	–	–	–			£18000[6]
453	–	– –	–		–			£15000[7]
454	–	Small Y.Head,[8]	As currency		–		£6600	
455	–	– ,[9] small legend	–		**1844**		£8800	
456	–	Y.H. chignon 'missing'[10]	–	**VIII**	–	£3600[11]		
457	–	– small legend,	–		**1845**		£3800	
458	–	– – heavy flan	–		–		£6800	
459	–	– – broad flan	–	**VIII**	–	£4500[11]	£4400	£30000
460	–	– – thin –	–		–		£4000	
461	–	– – –	–	**IX**	–	£7200[11]		

1: Smaller obv. lettering. 2: Reads: 'Dirige'. 3: Thin flan (.66oz), raised edge.

4: From among all 'Una & lion' £5 piece patterns these coins – having small Y.H. bearing full titles with plain rear fillet (the 'um' of Britanniarum directly adjacent to chignon) & thick border beads – were undoubtedly pattern crowns. They are only known paired with a rev. reading 'Dirigit' having the same thick border beads. Edged pieces have crown-sized raised letters. 5: weighs 1.71oz (raised edge). 6: weighs 1.262oz (raised edge). 7: weighs 1.262oz. 8: 'Una' head puncheon with plain fillets.

9: Copper penny head puncheon. 10: Hair below chignon incomplete. 11: Incuse edge.

Des: William Wyon

Obverse 1

Dies ↑↓

Des: William Dyce

Reverse A

No.	Dies		DATE ENDS mdccc&	Raised EDGE YEAR	DATE	P PROOF	E PROOF PLAIN EDGE	G GOLD PLAIN EDGE	W WHITE METAL P.Edge
470	**1 A**	Plain bodice	xlvi		**1846**		£6750		
471	–		xlvii	Undecimo	**1847**	900.00	£1250	£38000	£2400
472	–	Edge bordered	–	–	–	£5600			
473	–		–	Septimo	–	£6800			
474	–		liii	–	**1853**	£4300	£6000		

Des: J.E.Boehm

Obverse 1

Des: B.Pistrucci

Reverse type

Rev. A
Underside of groundline well-defined.

Rev C
Underside of groundline forms lines.

Rev. B
Compact undulating streamer.

No.	Dies		DATE	MINT STATE	P PROOF
480	**1 A**		**1887**	38.00	270.00
481	–		**1888**	115.00	
482	**1 B**	narrow date	–	75.00	
483	**1 A**		**1889**	50.00	
484	**1 C**		–	60.00	
485	**1 A**		**1890**	57.00	
486	–		**1891**	62.00	
487	–		**1892**	70.00	

Patterns

No.	Designer	OBV.	REV.	DATE	P PROOF
490	L.Wyon	Veiled bust	As currency	1888	£10500
491	–	– with 'L.C.W.'	–	–	£10000
492	–	–	'Five shillings' & St. George	1890	£12000
493	J.Boehm	'Jubilee' bust	–	–	£12000

Des: T.Brock

Obverse type

Des: B.Pistrucci

Reverse type

Obv. 1
'T' of 'Victoria' to bead.

Obv. 2
'T' of 'Victoria' to space.

Obv. 3
Border beads further from legend.

Rev. E
Diffused level streamer.

Rev. A
Single line beneath streamer.

Rev. B
Small design. Very thick streamer.

Rev. C
Undulating even streamer.

Rev. D
Thick top line. Cape closer to border.

No.	Dies	Raised EDGE YEAR	DATE	MINT STATE	P PROOF
500	**1 A**	LVI	1892		£11500[1]
501	–	–	1893	110.00	330.00
502	–	LVII	–	*	
503	**1 B**	LVI	–	215.00	
504	–	LVII	–	*	
505	**2 A**	LVI	–	125.00	310.00
506	–	LVII	–	235.00	
507	**1 C**	–	1894	210.00	
508	–	LVIII	–	*	
509	**2 C**	LVII	–	160.00	
510	–	LVIII	–	125.00	

1: Reads 'Reg' instead of 'Regina'.

No.	Dies	Raised EDGE YEAR	DATE	MINT STATE
511	**1 A**	**LVIII**	**1895**	*
512	–	**LIX**	–	130.00
513	**2 A**	**LVIII**	–	115.00
514	–	**LIX**	–	130.00
515	–	–	**1896**	*
516	–	**LX**	–	145.00
517	**1 D**	**LIX**	–	280.00
518	–	**LX**	–	*
519	**2 D**	**LIX**	–	300.00
520	–	**LX**	–	110.00
521	–	–	**1897**	110.00
522	–	**LXI**	–	105.00
523	–	–	**1898**	*
524	–	**LXII**	–	170.00
525	**2 E**	**LXI**	–	310.00
526	–	**LXII**	–	170.00
527	**3 E**	–	–	220.00
528	**2 E**	–	**1899**	135.00
529	–	**LXIII**	–	135.00
530	**3 E**	**LXII**	–	155.00
531	–	**LXIII**	–	155.00
532	**2 E**	–	**1900**	190.00
533	**3 E**	–	–	105.00
534	–	**LXIV**	–	110.00

Note: All edges are read with obv. uppermost. Edge dates vary in size.

DOUBLEFLORINS

Des: J.E.Boehm

Obverse type

Des: L.C.Wyon

Reverse type

Obv. 1
Cross on crown points to space.

Obv. 2
Cross on crown points to bead.

Rev. A
Harp's cross points to space.

Rev. B
Harp's cross to bead. Small sceptre cross.

Rev. C
Harp's cross to bead. Sceptre cross forms square.

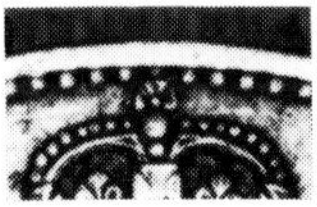

Rev. D
Harp's cross overlaps beads.

P

No.	Dies		DATE	MINT STATE	PROOF[1]
540	**1 A**	Roman 'I' in date	**1887**	35.00	180.00
541	**2 B**	Arabic '1' in date	–	30.00	160.00
542	–		**1888**	50.00	
543	–	reads: 'RIA' – broken serif [2]	–	90.00	
544	**2 C**		**1889**	45.00	
545	–	reads: 'RIA' – broken serif [2]	–	110.00	
546	**2 D**		**1890**	48.00	

1: 1887 proofs have broad even rims forming a distinct edge. 2: No lower left serif 'I'.

Pattern

P

No.	Designer	OBV.	REV.	DATE	PROOF
547	J.Boehm	'Jubilee' bust	'Doubleflorin' & shields	**1890**	£3750

HALFCROWNS

Des: W.Wyon

Des: J.Merlen

Obverse type *Dies* ↑↓ Reverse type

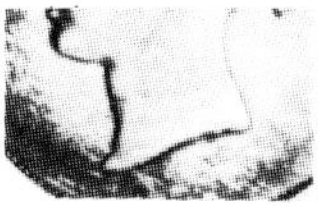

Obv. 1
One ornate & one plain fillet.

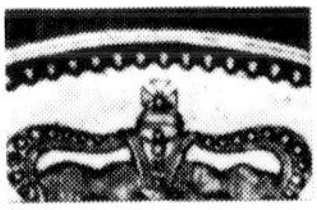

Rev. A
Small cross well away from beads.

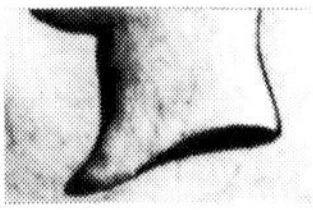

Obv. 2
Plain fillets. Bulky tip to truncation.

Rev. B
Medium cross. Foliage away from legend.

Obv. 3
'I' of 'Dei' to bead. 'I' of 'Ria' to space.

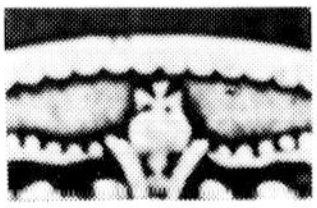

Rev. C
Small cross. Foliage near to legend.

Obv. 4
'I' of 'Dei' to space. 'I' of 'Ria' to space.

Rev. D
Large cross. Space between 'Gina' & 'Fid'.

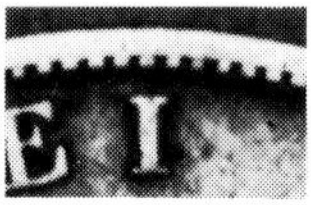

Obv. 5
'I' of 'Dei' to bead. 'I' of 'Ria' to bead.

No.	Dies		DATE	MINT STATE	P PROOF	E PROOF PLAIN EDGE	G GOLD PLAIN EDGE
560	**1 B**	'W.W.' in relief	**1839**	£2150	£1300	500.00	
561	**2 A**	–	–			£1700	
562	–	'W.W.' incuse	–	£1850	£1600	£1400	
563	**2 B**	–	**1840**	500.00			
564	–	no 'W.W.' hereonwards	**1841**	750.00			
565	–		**1842**	180.00			
566	–		**1843**	500.00			
567	– [1]		**1844**	160.00			
568	– [1]		**1845**	155.00			
569	– [1]		**1846**	190.00			
570	–		**1848**	850.00			
571	–	last '8' over '6'	–	775.00			
572	–	last '8' over '7'	–	950.00			
573	–		**1849**	260.00			
574	–	small date	–	350.00			
575	–		**1850**	245.00	680.00		
576	–		**1853**		830.00		
577	**1 B**		**1862**		£2250	£1850	
578	–		**1864**		£1700	£1750	
579	**3 C** [1]		**1874**	120.00	650.00	870.00	£10000
580	–		**1875**	137.00	670.00	£1250	
581	–		**1876**	145.00			
582	–	'6' over '5'	–	300.00			
583	–		**1877**	150.00			
584	–		**1878**	155.00	820.00		
585	–		**1879**	270.00	920.00		
586	**4 C**		–	230.00			
587	**4 D**		–	*	950.00		
588	**5 C**		**1880**	195.00	820.00		
589	**5 D**		–	150.00	*		
590	**4 D**		**1881**	145.00	*	*	
591	**5 D**		–	150.00	670.00	£1200	
592	–		**1882**	155.00			
593	–		**1883**	120.00			
594	– [1]		**1884**	130.00			
595	–		**1885**	125.00	670.00		
596	–		**1886**	130.00	£1300		
597	–		**1887**	160.00	900.00		

1: These coins exist either plain '4' or '4' with an upper serif.

Notes: Obv. 2 was retouched during 1840 and some coins exhibit slightly different profiles. Halfcrowns dated other than those above – principally 1861, 1866 1868 & 1871 – are sterling silver counterfeits from 'engraved-worn' steel dies bearing a portrait unlike any listed and probably of Edwardian origin.

Patterns

No.	Des.	OBV.	REV.	DATE	P PROOF	E PROOF PLAIN EDGE	G GOLD PLAIN EDGE
630	W.Wyon	Y.H. 'W.W.' 2 ornate fillets,	As currency	1839		£1800	
631	–	Small Y.H.[1] 2 plain	– –	–	£2600	£2500	
632	–	– 1 –	– –	–		£3200	
633	–	Y.H.[2]	Pistrucci's 'St. George'	1875		£3500	
634	L.Wyon	Coronetted head,	–	–		£3200	
635	–	–	W.Wyon's[3] –	1876		£2200	£5500
636	–	Veiled bust,	Crowned shield	1884	£2700		

1: Similar to the copper halfpenny puncheon.
2: This piece has date on both sides.
3: 'St. George' faces spectator's left with no exurge. Adapted from the Prince Albert medal.

Des: J.Boehm

Obverse type

Des: L.C.Wyon

Reverse type

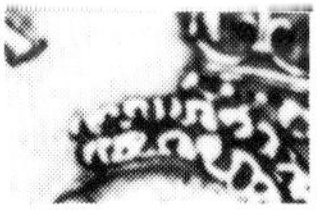

Obv. 1
Lace open at front of veil.

Obv. 2
Lace closed at front of veil.

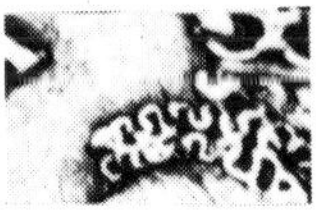

Obv. 3
'Tuft' at front of crown ermine.

Rev. A
Cross edges curved with large pearl. Chain is below arches.

Rev. B
Cross edges straight with small pearl. Chain is below arches.

Rev. C
Large cross with bold straight edges. Chain touches arches.

No.	Dies	DATE	MINT STATE	P PROOF
640	**1 A**	**1887**	17.00	
641	**2 A**	–	15.00	110.00
642	–	**1888**	43.00	650.00
643	–	**1889**	70.00	
644	**2 B**	–	95.00	
645	**3 A**	–	110.00	
646	**3 B**	–	75.00	
647	**3 C**	–	40.00	
648	–	**1890**	46.00	
649	–	**1891**	50.00	
650	–	**1892**	52.00	

Patterns

No.	Designer	OBV.	REV.	DATE	P PROOF
651	J.Boehm	'Jubilee' bust	'Halfcrown' & shield	**1890**	£3000
652	—	Diademed head	—	—	£3200

Des: T.Brock

Obverse type

Des: E.Poynter

Reverse type

Obv. 1 1st. 'I' of 'Victoria' to space.

Obv. 2 1st. 'I' of 'Victoria' to bead.

Rev. A Small design. Straight letter bases.

Rev. B Large design. Indented letter bases.

No.	Dies	DATE	MINT STATE	P PROOF
660	**1 A**	**1893**	45.00	
661	**2 A**	—	85.00	
662	**1 B**[1]	—	*	
663	**2 B**	—	*	115.00
664	**1 B**	**1894**	105.00	
665	**2 B**	—	65.00	
666	**1 B**	**1895**	*	
667	**2 B**	—	58.00	
668	**2 A**	**1896**	90.00	
669	**2 B**	—	48.00	
670	—	**1897**	42.00	
671	—	**1898**	50.00	
672	—	**1899**	45.00	
673	—	**1900**	43.00	
674	—	**1901**	50.00	

1: Rev. 'B' varies slightly in size each year but being pantographically enlarged, produces no die varieties.

*: to be confirmed.

FLORINS

Des: W.Wyon

Des: W.Dyce

Obverse 1 Dies ↑↓ Reverse A

No.	Dies			DATE	MINT STATE	P PROOF	E PROOF PLAIN EDGE	G GOLD PLAIN EDGE
680	**1 A**	**'WW'**,	beads not encircled	**1848**		680.00	420.00	£8500
681	–	–	beads encircled	**1849**	80.00			
682	–	–	obliterated by circle	–	95.00			

Patterns Dated 1848

No.	Designer	Obverse	Reverse	Reverse Legend				E PROOF PLAIN EDGE
690	W.Wyon	As Obv. '1'	As Rev. 'A'	One dime,	One tenth of a pound			570.00
691	–	–	'VR' cypher	One florin,		–	1	460.00
692	–	–	–	– ,	Two shillings		2	460.00
693	–	–	–	One centum,	One tenth of a pound		3	460.00
694	–	–	–	One decade,		–	5	460.00
695	–	–	Oak wreath	One florin,		–		460.00
696	–	–	–	One decade,	100 milles	–	6	460.00
697	–	–	–	One centum,	–	–	4	460.00
698	–	Y.H. Laur.	As Rev. 'A'	One florin,		–		520.00
699	–	–	–	One dime,		–		520.00
700	–	–	'VR' cypher	One florin,		–		420.00
701	–	–	–	–	Two shillings			420.00
702	–	–	–	One centum,	One tenth of a pound			420.00
703	–	–	–	One decade,		–		420.00
704	–	–	Oak wreath	One florin,		–		420.00
705	–	–	–	One decade,	100 milles	–		420.00
706	–	–	–	One centum,	–	–		420.00
707	–	Y.H. Plain	As Rev. 'A'	One florin,		–		520.00
708	–	–	–	One dime,		–		520.00
709	–	–	'VR' cypher	One florin,		–		420.00
710	–	–	–	–	Two shillings			420.00
711	–	–	–	One centum,	One tenth of a pound			420.00
712	–	–	–	One decade,		–		420.00
713	–	–	Oak wreath	One florin,		–		420.00
714	–	–	–	One decade,	100 milles	–		420.00
715	–	–	–	One centum,	–	–		420.00

Note: Reverses 1&2, 3&4, 5&6 combine as 3 different mules with edge date 'septimo'.

Des: W.Wyon. Des: W.Dyce.

Obverse type Dies ↑↓ Reverse type

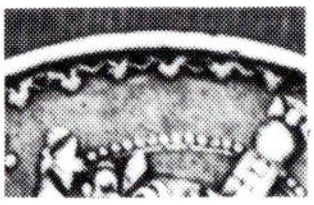

Obv. 1
48 border trefoils. **'Brit'.** crown 13½mm. **'WW'.** wide 'c c c'.

Rev. A
Top cross does not touch border beads.

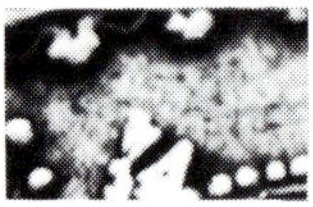

Obv. 2
48 trefoils. **'Brit'.** **'WW'.** cross incomplete & 14mm. close 'ccc'.

Rev. B
Top cross overlaps border beads.

Obv. 3
48 trefoils. **'WW'**, **'Britt'** hereonwards.

Obv. 7
33 trefoils. 7 jewels in centre of cross.

Obv. 4
41 trefoils. No **'WW'** hereonwards.

Obv. 8
33 trefoils. Head 1mm larger. Plait further from ear.

Obv. 5
38 trefoils.

Obv. 9
33 small trefoils forming longer arcs.

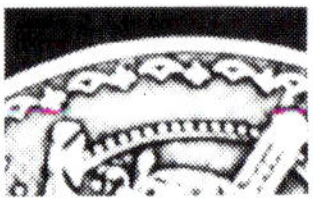

Obv. 6
33 trefoils. 8 jewels in centre of cross-patee, as preceding.

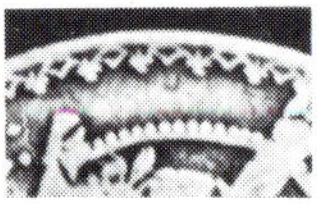

Obv. 10
46 trefoils.

No.	Dies		No. Tre-foils	DATE ENDS mdccc&	DATE	MINT STATE	P PROOF	E PROOF PLAIN EDGE
720	**1 A**		**48**	li.	**1851**		£2250	£2000
721	–		–	lii.	**1852**	100.00	550.00	
722	–	last 'i' over stop	–	lii.	–	170.00		
723	–		–	liii.	**1853**	*		
724	–		–	liii	–	177.00	450.00	
725	–	last 'i' over 'i'	–	liii	–	165.00		
726	–		–	liv	**1854**	£1600		
727	–		–	lv	**1855**	125.00		
728	–		–	lvi	**1856**	120.00		
729	–		–	lvii	**1857**	100.00	620.00	
730	–		–	lviii	**1858**	100.00	*	
731	**2 A**[1]		–	lviii	–	120.00	750.00	

1: Middle 'c' points to arch, not trefoil as previously but with cross-patée complete.

No.	Dies		No. Tre-foils	DATE ENDS mdccc&	Max Die No.	Prf. Die No.	DATE	MINT STATE	P PROOF	E PROOF PLAIN EDGE
732	**2 A** [1]		**48**	lix.			**1859**	115.00		
733	—	'm' over inverted 'm'	—	lix.			—	280.00		
734	**2 A**		—	lix			—	160.00		
735	—		—	lix.			—	115.00		
736	—		—	lx.			**1860**	150.00		
737	—	no colon after 'Brit'	—	lxii			**1862**	470.00	£1200	£1100
738	—		—	lxiii			**1863**	600.00	*	£1150
739	—		—	lxiv	73		**1864**	117.00		
740	—	Heavy flan (.475 oz)	—	lxiv	40	47	—	700.00	920.00	
741	—		—	lxv	54		**1865**	125.00		
742	—		—	lxv:	51		—	155.00		
743	—		—	lxvi	32		**1866**	140.00		
744	—		—	lxvi:			—	*		
745	—		—	lxvii	9		**1867**	280.00		
746	**3 A**		—	lxvii		non	—		850.00	830.00
747	—		—	lxviii	30		**1868**	235.00		
748	**3 B**		—	lxviii	12		—	125.00		
749	**3 A**		—	lxix	16		**1869**	290.00	*	
750	**3 B**		—	lxix	19	*	—	145.00	600.00	
751	**3 A**		—	lxx			**1870**	*		
752	**3 B**		—	lxx	27	35	—	120.00	900.00	
753	**3 A**		—	lxxi	68		**1871**	115.00	*	*
754	**3 B**		—	lxxi	64	43	—	107.00	700.00	730.00
755	**3 A**		—	lxxii	28		**1872**	145.00		
756	**3 B**		—	lxxii	156		—	105.00		
757	—		—	lxxiii	274	*	**1873**	105.00	600.00	
758	—		—	lxxiv	62		**1874**	115.00		
759	—	'u' over 'ii' [2]	—	lxxiv	30		—	270.00		
760	—		—	lxxv	88		**1875**	115.00		
761	—		—	lxxvi	50		**1876**	122.00		
762	— [3]		—	lxxvii	61		**1877**	125.00		
763	—	No 'WW'	—	lxxvii.			—	350.00		
764	**4 B** [4]	—	**41**	lxxvii.	68		—	140.00		
765	— [5]	—	—	lxxviii	95	73	**1878**	120.00	850.00	
766	—	—	—	lxxix			**1879**	470.00		
767	**3 B**		**48**	lxxix			—	130.00		
768	—	reads: 'Briit'	—	lxxix			—	190.00		
769	**5 B**		**38**	lxxix			—	120.00	730.00	
770	**6 B**		**33**	lxxx			**1880**	310.00		
771	**7 B**		—	lxxx			—	120.00	700.00	
772	—		—	lxxxi			**1881**	95.00	820.00	900.00
773	—	reads: 'xxxi'	—	lxxxi			—	90.00		

1: Head as Obv. 2 but with cross-patée complete.
2: Only known having die numbers 29 & 30, the latter being rarer.
3: Die number 8 is below bust & not shoulder.
4: Die numbers on these pieces occur either above 1st. or 2nd. arc to the right of brooch. Pieces showing no die numbers are from weakly struck or filled dies.
5: Die numbers on 1878 pieces are always above the 2nd. arc to right of brooch.
*: to be confirmed.

Note: Date endings occur with stop, without stop or with colon.

No.	Dies	No. Tre-foils	DATE ENDS mdccc&	DATE	MINT STATE	P PROOF
774	**8 B**	**33**	lxxxiii	**1883**	87.00	
775	–	–	lxxxiv	**1884**	90.00	
776	–	–	lxxxv	**1885**	130.00	*
777	**9 B**	–	lxxxv	–	95.00	620.00
778	–	–	lxxxvi	**1886**	95.00	650.00
779	–	–	lxxxvii	**1887**	*	
780	**10 B**	**46**	lxxxvii	–	155.00	750.00

PATTERN

No.	Designer	OBV.	REV.	DATE	P PROOF
790	L.C.Wyon	Coronetted head,	W.Wyon's 'St. George'[1]	**1876**	£2200

1: As halfcrown pattern of 1876 but lighter flan with 'St. George' facing left & no exurge.

Des: J.E.Boehm

Obverse type

Des: L.C.Wyon

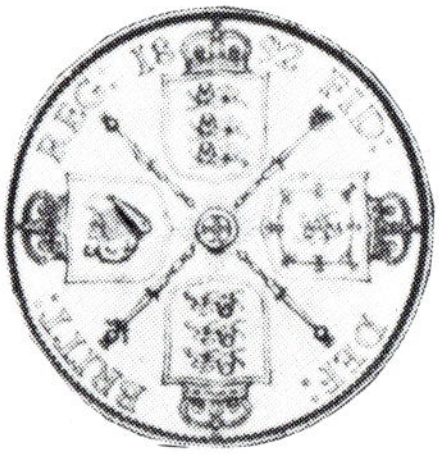

Reverse type

Obv. 1
'I' of 'Dei' to space, large capital 'J' in initials 'J.E.B.'

Obv. 2
'I' of 'Dei' left of bead. Small 'italic' 'J' in initials.

Obv. 3
Truncation close to beads.

Rev. A
Harp's cross to space. Date's cross to bead.

Rev. B
Harp's cross to bead. Date's cross to space.

Rev. C
Harp & date crosses both to spaces.

Rev. D
Harp & date crosses almost to beads.

No.	Dies	DATE	MINT STATE	P PROOF[2]
810	**1 A**[1]	**1887**	17.00	65.00
811	**2 A**	–	12.00	*
812	–	**1888**	90.00	
813	**3 A**	–	30.00	

P

No.	Dies	DATE	MINT STATE	PROOF
814	**3 B**	**1889**	90.00	
815	**3 C**	–	33.00	
816	–	**1890**	210.00	
817	**3 D**	–	115.00	
818	**3 C**	**1891**	270.00	
819	–	**1892**	320.00	800.00

1: There are several variations of these capital 'J' type initials for obv. 1 & all have broad rims.

2: 1887 proofs have broad even rims forming a distinct edge.

Pattern

P

No.	Designer	OBV.	REV.	DATE	PROOF
820	L.C.Wyon	'Jubilee' bust	'florin' & shields	**1891**	£2200

Des: T.Brock

Obverse type

Des: E.Poynter

Reverse type

Obv. 1
1st. 'I' of 'Victoria' to space.

Obv. 2
1st. 'I' of 'Victoria' to bead.

Rev. A
L.H. leg of 'H' to bead.

Rev. B
L.H. leg of 'H' to space.

P

No.	Dies	DATE	MINT STATE	PROOF
830	**1 A**	**1893**	40.00	80.00
831	**2 A**	–	*	90.00
832	**1 A**	**1894**	*	
833	**1 B**	–	75.00	
834	**2 A**	–	*	
835	**2 B**	–	52.00	
836	**1 A**	**1895**	80.00	
837	**1 B**	–	*	
838	**2 A**	–	55.00	
839	**2 B**	–	*	

*: to be confirmed.

No.	Dies	DATE	MINT STATE
840	**1 A**	**1896**	*
841	**1 B**	–	70.00
842	**2 A**	–	95.00
843	**2 B**	–	47.00
844	–	**1897**	43.00
845	–	**1898**	50.00
846	–	**1899**	40.00
847	–	**1900**	42.00
848	–	**1901**	47.00

SHILLINGS

Des: W.Wyon

Des: J.Merlen

Obverse type *Dies* ↑↓ Reverse type

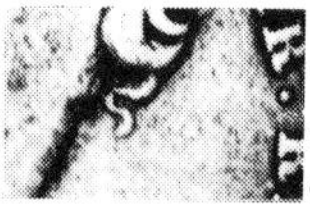

Obv. 1
'WW' in relief. Small slim head. Chignon ends in loose curl.

Obv. 2
No 'WW', base of 'E' longer than top. 13 beads between 'A's.

Obv. 3
Base of 'E's equal to top. Upright of 'B' to bead, 11 from A to A.

Obv. 4
'I' of 'Vict' to bead. Upright of 'B' & 'I' of 'niar' to space.

Obv. 5
'I' of 'Vict' to space. 8 beads between 'A's Short serifs in 'I's.

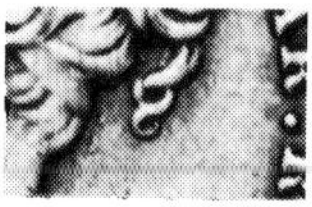

Obv. 6
'I' of 'Gratia' to bead. 'I's have long serifs. 'O' to bead.

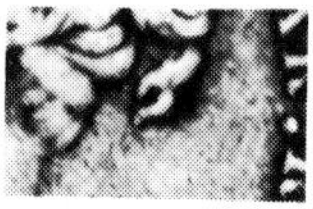

Obv. 7
Chignon end tapers to faint circle. Truncation tip rounded.

Rev. A
Cross on crown right of bead. Noticeable gap between 'L's.

Rev. B
Cross on crown right of bead. Gap closed between 'L's.

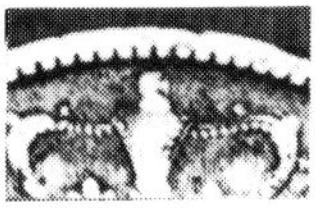

Rev. C
Cross on crown to space. Base of crown more shallow.

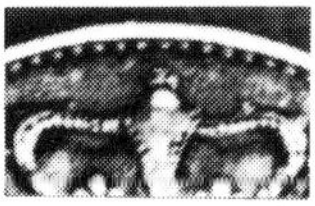

Rev. D
Cross on crown to bead. Long thick line below 'shilling'.

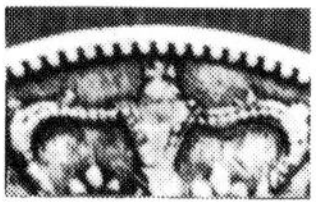

Rev. E
Only known for 1882. Cross on crown slightly left of bead.

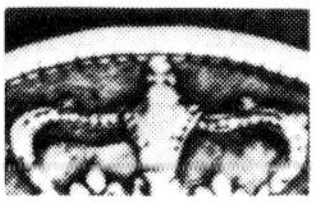

Rev. F
Cross touches beads. Short thick line below 'shilling'.

No.	Dies		Max Die No.	Prf. Die No.	DATE	MINT STATE	P PROOF	E PROOF PLAIN EDGE
850	**1 A**				**1838**	85.00	420.00	
851	–				**1839**	92.00		250.00
852	**2 A**	with 'WW'			–			140.00
853	–	no 'WW'			–	70.00	630.00	220.00
854	–				**1840**	215.00	650.00	
855	–				**1841**	90.00		
856	–				**1842**	70.00	570.00	
857	–				**1843**	95.00		
858	–				**1844**	68.00		
859	–				**1845**	90.00		
860	–				**1846**	82.00		
861	–	'8' over '6'			**1848**	280.00		
862	–				**1849**	82.00		
863	–				**1850**	£1350		
864	–	'50' over '46'			–	£1600		
865	–				**1851**	480.00	920.00	
866	–				**1852**	70.00		
867	–				**1853**	67.00	240.00	
868	–				**1854**	650.00		
869	–				**1855**	68.00		
870	–				**1856**	68.00		
871	–				**1857**	68.00		
872	–	reads: 'F:ᗡ:'			–	500.00		
873	–				**1858**	68.00		
874	–	'8' over '6'			–	125.00		
875	**4 A**				–	270.00		
876	**2 A**	'9' over '8' [1]			**1859**	150.00		
877	–				–	*		
878	**3 A**				–	170.00		
879	**4 A**				–	70.00		
880	–	'9' over '8'			–	170.00		
881	–				**1860**	120.00		
882	–				**1861**	140.00		
883	–				**1862**	215.00		
884	–				**1863**	270.00		
885	–	'3' over '2' or '1'			–	*		
886	–		80		**1864**	85.00		
887	–	large '4'	41		–	110.00		
888	–		130		**1865**	82.00		
889	–	'5' over '3'	29		–	145.00		
890	–		70	70	**1866**	85.00	500.00	
891	–	reads: 'Bbitanniar'	63		–	*		

1: This coin has Obv. 3 type 'E's.

*: to be confirmed.

No.	Dies		Max Die No.	Prf. Die No.	DATE	MINT STATE	P PROOF	E PROOF PLAIN EDGE
892	**4 A**		37		**1867**	90.00		
893	**4 B**[1]		18		–	240.00		
894	**5 A**				–	*		
895	**5 B**		17	non	–	330.00	550.00	620.00
896	–		54		**1868**	82.00		
897	–		15		**1869**	125.00		
898	–		20		**1870**	120.00		
899	–		56	19	**1871**	60.00	480.00	520.00
900	–		155		**1872**	50.00		
901	–		141		**1873**	50.00		
902	–		76		**1874**	55.00		
903	–	crosslet '4'	15		–	85.00		
904	–		74		**1875**	57.00		
905	–		36		**1876**	100.00		
906	– [2]		69		**1877**	60.00		
907	–		42		**1878**	140.00	*	
908	**6 B**[3]		76	*	–	62.00	430.00	
909	**5 B**		12		**1879**	240.00	*	
910	**6 B**[4]		26	*	–	95.00	440.00	
911	– [5]		non		–	*		
912	**7 C**				–	72.00		
913	–				**1880**	125.00	*	*
914	**7 D**				–	60.00	370.00	540.00
915	**7 C**[6]				**1881**	115.00		*
916	**7 D**				–	50.00	430.00	630.00
917	–	'Shilling' more spaced			–	190.00		
918	**7 E**				**1882**	120.00		
919	**7 D**				**1883**	95.00		
920	–	'pointed' 'A's[7]			–	50.00		
921	–	–			**1884**	50.00	*	
922	**7 F**	–			–	125.00	500.00	
923	–	–			**1885**	45.00	480.00	
924	–	–			**1886**	50.00	600.00	
925	–	–			**1887**	85.00	510.00	

1: Rev. 'B' for this year exhibits a small dot between ribbons above die number.
2: Coins of this date with no die number are believed counterfeit.
3: Die '31' of this type is also known with a tiny '2' within lower circle of last '8'.
4: Die '6' of this type has 'H' of 'Shilling' doubled.
5: This piece may exist showing very faint die number.
6: Rev. 'C' is paired with an obv. '7' having slightly smaller head.
7: 'A's protrude above line of legend which is slightly further from beads.

Note: On 1878 shillings from dies 74–76 & all 1879 pieces the 'S' in 'Shilling' varies in size.

*: to be confirmed.

Patterns

No.	Designer	OBV.	REV.	DATE	P PROOF	E PROOF PLAIN EDGE
960	W.Wyon	Y.Head	As currency but lined	**1839**	850.00	
961	Wiener	Wreathed head. no initials.	As currency	**1863**		760.00
962	–	– 'C.H.W' raised.	–	–		760.00
963	–	Coronetted head, –	–	–		780.00
964	–	– 'C.H.W' incuse.	–	–		780.00
965	W.Wyon	Y.Head	Pistrucci's St. George	**1875**	£1500	£1500
966	–	–	–	none	780.00	
967	L.Wyon	Coronetted head,	–	**1875**	950.00	
968	W.Wyon	Y.Head	Crowned shield in garter	**1880**		950.00

Des: J.E.Boehm

Obverse type

Des: L.C.Wyon

Reverse type

Obv. 1
Small head. Truncation well away from beads.

Obv. 2
Large head. Truncation almost touching beads.

Obv. 3
Large head. Truncation slightly away from beads.

Rev. A
Small garter letters. 'Q' has long loopless tail.

Rev. B
Large garter letters. 'Q' has almost no tail.

Rev. C
Medium garter letters. 'Q' has curved looped tail.

Rev. D
'U' further from shield. No extra line along crown.

No.	Dies	DATE	MINT STATE	P PROOF
980	**1 A**	**1887**	28.00	*
981	**1 B**	–	12.00	*
982	**1 C**	–	7.00	48.00
983	– '8' over '7'	**1888**	29.00	
984	– [1]	**1889**	290.00	
985	**1 D**	–	350.00	
986	**2 D**	–	25.00	
987	**3 D**	–	38.00	350.00

1: Also known with '9' close to '8' as rev. D.

No.	Dies	DATE	MINT STATE	P PROOF
988	**3 D**	**1890**	30.00	560.00
989	–	**1891**	35.00	560.00
990	–	**1892**	38.00	

Patterns

No.	Designer	OBV.	REV.	DATE	P PROOF
1000	J.Boehm	'Jubilee' bust	'One shilling' & shield	**1887**	£1150
1001	–	–	– –	**1888**	£1200
1002	–	–	– with scroll	–	£1250
1003	–	Large 'Jubilee' bust	– & shield	–	£1150

Des: T.Brock

Obverse type

Des: E.Poynter

Reverse type

Obv. 1
Small letters.
'I' of 'Vict'
to bead.

Obv. 2
Large letters.
'I' of 'Vict'
to space.

Rev. D
L.H. crown's cross
points to bead.
Large rose.

Rev. A
L.H. crown's cross
points to space.
small rose & lip.

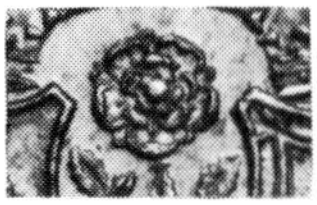

Rev. B
L.H. crown's cross
points to bead.
small rose & lip.

Rev. C
L.H. crown's cross
points to space.
small rose with line.

No.	Dies	DATE	MINT STATE	P PROOF
1010	**1 A**	**1893**	22.00	
1011	**2 A**	–	30.00	70.00
1012	**1 A**	**1894**	*	
1013	**1 B**	–	95.00	
1014	**2 A**	–	45.00	
1015	**2 B**	–	30.00	
1016	–	**1895**	*	
1017	**2 C**	–	80.00	
1018	**2 D**	–	30.00	
1019	**2 C**	**1896**	95.00	
1020	**2 D**	–	30.00	

*: to be confirmed.

No.	Dies	DATE	MINT STATE
1021	**2 D**	**1897**	24.00 [1]
1022	–	**1898**	27.00
1023	–	**1899**	24.00
1024	–	**1900**	24.00
1025	–	**1901**	28.00

1: Also occurs with '7' almost touching '9' & '7' close to '9'.

TENPENCE

Pattern

No.	Designer	OBV.	REV.	DATE	E PROOF PLAIN EDGE
1026	L.Wyon	Coronetted head	Shield in wreath	**1867**	500.00

SIXPENCES

Des: W.Wyon Des: J.Merlen

Obv. type Dies ↑↓ Rev. type

Obv. 1
Flat nape, thin curl.
'I' of 'Gratia' to bead.
10 beads from 'A' s.

Obv. 2
Slight bulge at nape.
'I' of 'Gratia' right of bead. 10 beads in 'A's.

Obv. 3
'D' of 'Dei' to space.
'I' of 'Gratia' to space.
9 beads from 'A's.

Obv. 4
'D' of 'Dei' to bead.
'I' of 'Gratia' to space.
8 beads from 'A's.

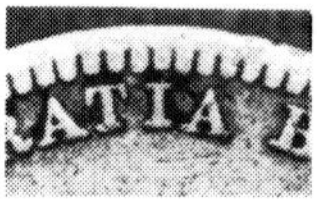

Obv. 5
Small head, long beads.
'I' of 'Gratia' to bead.
8 beads from 'A's.

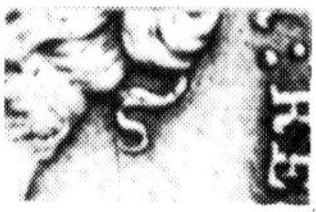

Obv. 6
Smaller shorter beads.
'I' of 'Gratia' to space.
11 beads from 'A's.

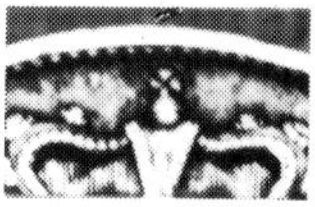

Rev. A
Very small beads.
Cross left of bead.
Date covers 12 beads.

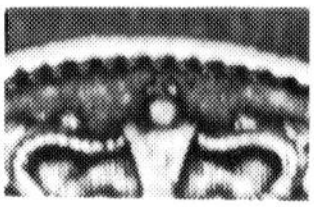

Rev. B
Large broad beads.
Cross right of bead.
Date covers 9 beads.

Rev. C
Wreath touches beads.
Cross left of bead.
Date covers 11 beads.

Rev. D
Faint cross touches left of bead.
Date covers 10 beads.

Rev. E
1882 only. Wreath touches left side.
Date covers 12 beads.

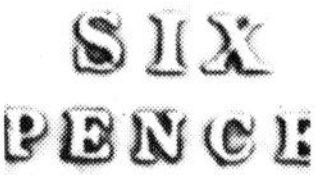

Rev. F
'Six-pence' wider.
Cross to space.
Date covers 11 beads.

No.	Dies		Max Die No.	Prf. Die No.	DATE	MINT STATE	P PROOF	E PROOF PLAIN EDGE
1030	**1 A**				**1838**	58.00	195.00	
1031	–				**1839**	57.00		140.00
1032	–				**1840**	67.00		
1033	–				**1841**	72.00		
1034	–				**1842**	62.00		
1035	–				**1843**	58.00		
1036	–				**1844**	56.00		
1037	–	Large '44'			–	105.00		
1038	–				**1845**	60.00		
1039	–				**1846**	62.00		
1040	–				**1847**	*		
1041	–				**1848**	230.00		
1042	–	'8' over '6'			–	210.00		
1043	–	'8' over '7'			–	300.00		
1044	–				**1850**	80.00		
1045	–	'5' over '3'			–	135.00		
1046	–	'G's have one serif [1]			**1851**	105.00		
1047	–	– both serifs			–	65.00		
1048	–	– one serif			**1852**	60.00		
1049	–	– both serifs			–	70.00		
1050	–				**1853**	55.00	190.00	
1051	–				**1854**	360.00		
1052	–				**1855**	57.00	270.00	
1053	–				**1856**	57.00		
1054	–	long line below 'Pence'			–	62.00		
1055	–				**1857**	60.00		
1056	–	long line below 'Pence'			–	65.00		
1057	–				**1858**	110.00		
1058	**2 A**				–	60.00	360.00	
1059	–				**1859**	58.00		
1060	–	'9' over '8'			–	70.00		
1061	–				**1860**	62.00		
1062	–				**1862**	180.00		
1063	–				**1863**	120.00		
1064	–	small date, plain '4'	12	2	**1864**	75.00	400.00	
1065	–	serif '4'	36		–	60.00		
1066	–	small date, serif '4'	41		–	95.00		
1067	–		32		**1865**	70.00		
1068	–		none		**1866**	300.00		
1069	–		59		–	58.00		
1070	–		19		**1867**	90.00	*	
1071	**3 A**		26	2	–	95.00	370.00	

1: The left inner serif is noticeably shorter, only occuring on obv. 1.

*: to be confirmed.

No.	Dies		Max Die No.	Prf. Die No.	DATE	MINT STATE	P PROOF	E PROOF PLAIN EDGE
1072	**2 A**		7		**1868**	125.00		
1073	**3 A**		17		–	110.00		
1074	–		19	17	**1869**	115.00	370.00	
1075	–		12	12	**1870**	120.00		410.00
1076	–		none	none	**1871**	75.00	440.00	
1077	–		54	14	–	55.00		410.00
1078	–		73		**1872**	53.00		
1079	–		124		**1873**	50.00		
1080	**3 B**		96		–	130.00		
1081	**3 C**		117		–	180.00		
1082	–	crosslet '4'	25		**1874**	52.00		
1083	**4 C**	–	48		–	55.00		
1084	–	plain '4'	60		–	95.00		
1085	**3 C**		74		**1875**	130.00		
1086	**4 C**		88		–	52.00		
1087	–		29		**1876**	110.00		
1088	–		none		**1877**	50.00		
1089	–		35		–	60.00		
1090	–		70	41	**1878**	52.00	370.00	
1091	–	'8' over '7'	30		–	130.00		
1092	–	reads: 'Dritanniar' [1]	6		–	400.00		
1093	–		21		**1879**	105.00		
1094	–				–	165.00	370.00	
1095	**4 D**				–	50.00		
1096	**5 D**				–	85.00		
1097	–				**1880**	65.00		
1098	**6 D**				–	37.00	340.00	
1099	–				**1881**	35.00	350.00	400.00
1100	–	large date			–	48.00		
1101	**6 E**				**1882**	90.00		
1102	**6 F**				**1883**	33.00		
1103	–				**1884**	32.00		
1104	–				**1885**	30.00	420.00	
1105	–				**1886**	32.00	420.00	
1106	–				**1887**	30.00	350.00	

1: Only known with die number '6' & this consignment was sent for use in Cyprus.

Patterns

No.	Designer	OBV.	REV.	DATE	P PROOF	E PROOF PLAIN EDGE	G GOLD PROOF
1140	W.Wyon	Y.Head	As currency but lined	**1840**	600.00		
1141	–	– as half sov. die,	As currency	**1841**			£3500
1142	–	–	'Half shilling' –	**1856**		720.00	
1143	–	–	'½ shilling' –	–		900.00	
1144	L.Wyon	Veiled bust	Cruciform shields	**1884**	750.00		

Des: J.Boehm

Obverse type

Des: L.Wyon

Reverse A

Obv. 1
'J.E.B.' on truncation. 'I' of 'Brit' to bead.

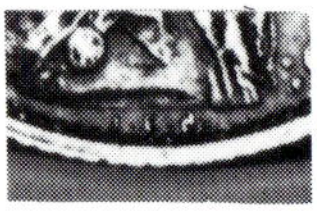

Obv. 2
'J.E.B.' off truncation. 'I' of 'Brit' to space.

No.	Dies		DATE	MINT STATE	P PROOF
1150	**1 A**		**1887**	35.00	40.00
1151	**2 A**		—	4.00	
1152	—	'r' of 'Victoria' over 'i'	—	25.00	
1153	—	'r' of 'Victoria' over 'v'	—	33.00	
1154	—	'r' of 'Victoria' over 'b'	—	30.00	

Pattern

No.	Designer	OBV.	REV.	DATE	P PROOF
1155	J.Boehm	'Jubilee' bust	'Six-pence' & shield	**1887**	900.00

Des: J.Boehm

Obverse 1

Des: L.Wyon

Reverse type

Rev. A
Small design. severed leaf on right side.

Rev. D
Right hand leaf almost covers a leaf. Left stem bent.

Rev. B
Medium-sized design. Joined leaf. Stem on left is angled.

Rev. E
No line under crown. Berries and leaves bolder.

Rev. C
Large design. Thin low outline under *fleur-de-lys*.

Note: Numerous design & die sinking differences exist before final adoption of rev. 'D'.
The above five reverses constitute the principal dies employed.
The enlarged obv. '1' illustration is simulated.

No.	Dies		DATE	MINT STATE	P PROOF
1160	**1 A**		**1887**	5.00	280.00
1161	–		**1888**	18.00	*
1162	**1 B**		–	17.00	430.00
1163	–	'1' over '1' in date	–	36.00	
1164	**1 C**		**1889**	28.00	
1165	**1 D**		–	16.00	
1166	–		**1890**	30.00	*
1167	**1 E**		–	18.00	310.00
1168	**1 D**		**1891**	22.00	
1169	–		**1892**	22.00	
1170	–		**1893**	£1000	

Des: T.Brock

Obverse type

Des: L.Wyon

Reverse type

Obv. 1
1st. 'I' of 'Victoria' to space.

Rev. A
Left ribbon end points to space.

Obv. 2
1st. 'I' of 'Victoria' to bead.

Rev. B
Left ribbon end points to bead.

No.	Dies	DATE	MINT STATE	P PROOF
1180	**1 A**	**1893**	16.00	45.00
1181	**2 A**	–	50.00	*
1182	–	**1894**	27.00	
1183	–	**1895**	22.00	
1184	–	**1896**	20.00	
1185	–	**1897**	18.00	
1186	– [1]	**1898**	20.00	
1187	**2 B**	**1899**	18.00	
1188	–	**1900**	16.00	
1189	– [2]	**1901**	16.00	

1: This year has larger date.
2: The '1' of date points to space as rev. A.
*: to be confirmed.

GROATS

Des: W.Wyon

Obverse 1

Dies ↑↑

Des: W.Wyon

Reverse A

No.	Dies [1]		DATE	MINT STATE	P PROOF	E PROOF PLAIN EDGE
1200	**1 A**		**1837**		370.00	370.00
1201	–		**1838**	17.00		180.00
1202	–	last '8' over horizontal '8'	–	38.00		
1203	–		**1839**	24.00		80.00
1204	–	small date	**1840**	22.00		
1205	–	large date	–	27.00		
1206	–	narrow '0' in date	–	45.00		
1207	–		**1841**	37.00		
1208	–	small 'N' in 'Pence'	–	70.00		
1209	–	last '1' in date over inverted '1'	–	50.00		
1210	–		**1842**	28.00		150.00
1211	–	'2' over '1'	–	47.00		
1212	–		**1843**	28.00		
1213	–	'4' over '5'	–	58.00		
1214	–	top stops of colons higher	–	50.00		
1215	–		**1844**	40.00		
1216	–		**1845**	28.00		
1217	–		**1846**	26.00		
1218	–	'7' over '6'	**1847**	60.00		
1219	–	small date	**1848**	25.00		
1220	–	large date	–	25.00		
1221	–	'8' over '6'	–	38.00		
1222	–	'8' over '7'	–	50.00		
1223	–	small date	**1849**	35.00		
1224	–	large date	–	35.00		
1225	–	'9' over '9'	–	55.00		
1226	–		**1851**	140.00		
1227	–		**1852**	250.00		
1228	-		**1853**	280.00	180.00	270.00
1229	–		**1854**	24.00		
1230	–	'5' over '3'	–	35.00		
1231	–	colon touches 'r' of 'niar'	–	55.00		
1232	–	extra stop under colon of 'niar'	–	55.00		
1233	–		**1855**	25.00		
1234	**3 A**		**1857**		400.00	
1235	**2 A**		**1862**			240.00

1: Obv. 2 & 3 are from the threepence series.

Note: Date sizes vary considerably.

Des: J.Boehm

Obverse 1

Des: W.Wyon

Reverse A

P

No.	Dies	DATE	MINT STATE	PROOF
1236	**1 A**	**1888**	35.00	270.00

THREEPENCES

Des: W.Wyon

Des: J.Merlen

Obv. type *Dies* ↑↓ Rev. type

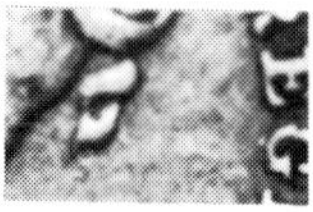

Obv. 1
Right leg of 1st. 'N' in 'Brit' to bead. 'G' has right serif.

Rev. A
Large border beads. Cross away from beads.

Obv. 2
Lowest hair wave covers top of ear. 'G' has left & right serif.

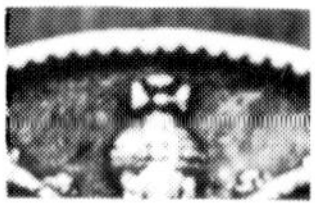

Rev. B
Small border beads. Cross nearer beads.

Obv. 3
Right leg of 1st. 'N' in 'Brit' to space. 'Victoria' close 'DG'.

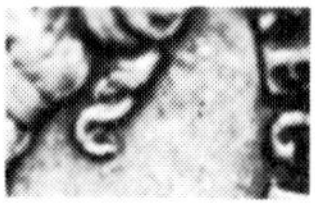

Obv. 4
Right leg of 1st. 'N' in 'Brit' to bead. Gap after 'Victoria'.

No.	Dies [1]		DATE	MINT STATE
1250	**1 A**		**1838**	38.00
1251	–		**1839**	60.00
1252	–		**1840**	42.00
1253	–		**1841**	52.00
1254	–		**1842**	75.00
1255	–		**1843**	30.00
1256	–		**1844**	42.00
1257	–		**1845**	28.00
1258	–	large date	–	47.00
1259	–		**1846**	75.00
1260	–		**1849**	58.00
1261	–		**1850**	33.00
1262	–		**1851**	38.00
1263	–	reads: '1551'	–	475.00
1264	–		**1853**	75.00
1265	–		**1854**	38.00

1: These coins are plain edged. 1842 & 1846 may only occur as Maundy issues.

No.	Dies		DATE	MINT STATE	E PROOF PLAIN EDGE
1266	**1 A**		**1855**	65.00	
1267	–	large '55'	–	55.00	
1268	–		**1856**	40.00	
1269	–		**1857**	35.00	
1270	–		**1858**	35.00	
1271	–	'8' over '6'	–	80.00	
1272	–	reads: 'Britanniab Begina'	–	450.00	
1273	–		**1859**	40.00	
1274	–	small '59'	–	32.00	
1275	–[1]		–	28.00	
1276	**2 A**		–	45.00	
1277	**1 A**		**1860**	120.00	
1278	**2 A**		–	28.00	
1279	–		**1861**	32.00	
1280	–		**1862**	42.00	
1281	–		**1863**	48.00	
1282	–		**1864**	35.00	
1283	–		**1865**	48.00	
1284	–		**1866**	32.00	
1285	**3 A**		–	150.00	
1286	**2 A**		**1867**	40.00	
1287	**2 B**		–	*	
1288	**3 A**		–	55.00	
1289	**3 B**		–	38.00	
1290	**2 A**		**1868**	35.00	
1291	–	reads: 'Rritanniar'	–	270.00	
1292	**2 B**		–	*	
1293	**3 A**		–	*	
1294	**3 B**		–	50.00	
1295	–		**1869**	60.00	
1296	–		**1870**	30.00	
1297	–		**1871**	35.00	
1298	–		**1872**	32.00	
1299	–		**1873**	22.00	
1300	–		**1874**	22.00	
1301	–		**1875**	22.00	
1302	–		**1876**	28.00	
1303	–	'6' over '5'	–	70.00	
1304	–		**1877**	25.00	
1305	–		**1878**	28.00	
1306	–		**1879**	25.00	*
1307	–	Hair heavily re-engraved	–	28.00	105.00
1308	**4 B**	large '3'	**1880**	30.00	
1309	–		**1881**	25.00	
1310	–		**1882**	40.00	

1: Head as obv. 1 (having top of ear visible), but obv. 2 type serifs to 'G'.

No.	Dies	DATE	MINT STATE	E PROOF PLAIN EDGE
1311	**4 B**	**1883**	18.00	
1312	–	**1884**	18.00	
1313	–	**1885**	17.00	
1314	–	**1886**	15.00	
1315	–	**1887**	18.00	105.00

Pattern

No.	Designer	OBV.	REV.	DATE	E PROOF PLAIN EDGE
1316	L.Wyon	Laureated head	As currency	**1868**	480.00

Des: J.Boehm

Obv. type

Des: L.Wyon

Rev. type

Obv. 1
7 pearls left side of crown. 2 dots each side of cross.

Obv. 2
1st. 'I' of 'Victoria' to bead. 2 lines each side of cross.

Obv. 3
1st. 'I' of 'Victoria' to space. 2 dots each side of cross.

Rev. A
Cross patée plain. Thin low outline under *fleur de lis*.

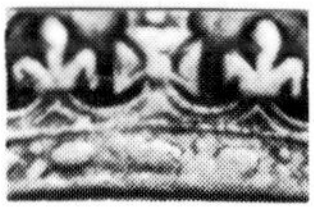

Rev. B
Cross patée has border. High outline under *fleur de lis*.

Rev. C
Thick cross patée border. Double line across crown.

No.	Dies	DATE	MINT STATE	E PROOF PLAIN EDGE
1330	**1 A**	**1887**	8.00	23.00
1331	**2 A**	–	5.00	*
1332	**1 A**	**1888**	*	
1333	**2 A**	–	28.00	
1334	**1 A**	**1889**	*	
1335	**1 B**	–	28.00	
1336	**2 A**	–	40.00	
1337	**2 B**	–	13.00	
1338	**3 A**	–	*	
1339	**3 B**	–	32.00	
1340	**3 A**	**1890**	40.00	
1341	**3 C**	–	13.00	
1342	**3 A**	**1891**	12.00	
1343	–	**1892**	14.00	
1344	–	**1893**	45.00	

Des: T.Brock

Obv. type

Des: L.Wyon

Rev. type

Obv. 1
2nd. 'I' of 'Victoria' to space.

Obv. 2
2nd. 'I' of 'Victoria' to bead.

Rev. A
Cross patée plain. Thin low outline under *fleur de lis.*

Rev. B
Pearls more distinct & different position to jewels below.

Rev. C
Ribbon 'unbalanced'. Right ribbon end thicker than left.

No.	Dies	DATE	MINT STATE	E PROOF PLAIN EDGE
1350	**1 A**	**1893**	14.00	27.00
1351	**2 A**	–	7.00	
1352	**1 A**	**1894**	18.00	
1353	**2 A**	–	17.00	
1354	–	**1895**	12.00	
1355	–	**1896**	11.00	
1356	–	**1897**	10.00	
1357	–	**1898**	10.00	
1358	**2 B**	**1899**	9.00	
1359	**2 A**	**1900**	9.00	
1360	**2 C**	**1901**	9.00	

TWOPENCES

Des: Wyon

Des: Merlen

Obv. 1 *Dies* ↑↓ Rev. A

No.	Dies[1]		DATE	MINT STATE
1370	**1 A**		**1838**	13.00
1371	–	last '8' reads: 'S'	–	28.00
1372	–		**1848**	15.00

1: Twopences & threehalfpences are plain edged.

THREEHALFPENCES

Des: Wyon | Des: Merlen

Obv. 1 *Dies* ↑↓ Rev. A

No.	Dies		DATE	MINT STATE	E PROOF PLAIN EDGE
1380	**1 A**		**1838**	18.00	
1381	–		**1839**	13.00	
1382	–		**1840**	30.00	
1383	–		**1841**	14.00	
1384	–		**1842**	22.00	
1385	–		**1843**	11.00	
1386	–	'43' over '34'	–	45.00	
1387	–		**1860**	35.00	
1388	–		**1862**	32.00	
1389	–		**1870**		280.00

MAUNDY SETS

Des: W.Wyon | Des: J.Merlen

Obverse 1 Reverse A

No.	Dies[1]		DATE	MINT STATE	E PROOF PLAIN EDGE	G GOLD PLAIN EDGE	3d Dies[2]
1400	**1 A**	Set of 4d, 3d, 2d & 1d	**1838**	45.00	240.00	£3800	1 A
1401	–	–	**1839**	45.00	150.00		–
1402	–	–	**1840**	48.00			–
1403	–	–	**1841**	55.00			–
1404	–	–	**1842**	42.00			–
1405	–	–	**1843**	42.00			–
1406	–	–	**1844**	42.00			–
1407	–	–	**1845**	42.00			–
1408	–	–	**1846**	42.00			–
1409	–	–	**1847**	42.00			–
1410	–	–	**1848**	42.00			–
1411	–	–	**1849**	47.00			–
1412	–	–	**1850**	42.00			–
1413	–	–	**1851**	42.00			–
1414	–	–	**1852**	42.00			–
1415	–	–	**1853**	42.00	200.00		–

1: These coins have proof-like surfaces & are plain edged.
2: These dies are from the threepence series.

No.	Dies [1]		DATE	MINT STATE	E PROOF PLAIN EDGE	3d Dies [2]
1416	**1 A**	Set of 4d, 3d, 2d & 1d	**1854**	42.00		1 A
1417	–	–	**1855**	48.00		–
1418	–	–	**1856**	42.00		–
1419	–	–	**1857**	42.00		–
1420	–	–	**1858**	42.00		–
1421	– [3]	–	**1859**	42.00		1,2 A
1422	–	–	**1860**	42.00		1 A
1423	– [4]	–	**1861**	42.00		–
1424	–	–	**1862**	42.00		2 A
1425	–	–	**1863**	48.00		–
1426	–	–	**1864**	45.00		–
1427	–	–	**1865**	48.00		–
1428	–	–	**1866**	45.00		–
1429	–	–	**1867**	45.00	230.00	–
1430	–	–	**1868**	45.00		3 B
1431	–	–	**1869**	48.00		–
1432	–	–	**1870**	42.00		–
1433	–	–	**1871**	42.00	290.00	–
1434	–	–	**1872**	42.00		–
1435	–	–	**1873**	42.00		–
1436	–	–	**1874**	42.00		–
1437	–	–	**1875**	42.00		–
1438	–	–	**1876**	42.00		–
1439	–	–	**1877**	42.00		–
1440	–	–	**1878**	42.00	230.00	–
1441	–	–	**1879**	42.00		–
1442	–	–	**1880**	42.00		4 B
1443	–	–	**1881**	42.00	230.00	–
1444	–	–	**1882**	42.00		–
1445	–	–	**1883**	42.00		–
1446	–	–	**1884**	42.00		–
1447	–	–	**1885**	42.00		–
1448	–	–	**1886**	42.00		–
1449		–	**1887**	70.00		–

1: These coins generally have proof-like surfaces & are plain edged.
2: These dies are from the threepence series.
3: 'Beitanniar' known on the twopence of this year.
4: '6' over '1' known on the twopence of this year.

Des: J.Boehm

Obverse 1

Des: L.Wyon

Reverse A

No.	Dies[1]		DATE	MINT STATE	E	3d Dies[2]
					PROOF PLAIN EDGE	
1470	**1 A**	Set of 4d, 3d, 2d & 1d	**1888**	52.00	210.00	2 B
1471	–	–	**1889**	45.00		
1472	–	–	**1890**	45.00		
1473	–	–	**1891**	45.00		
1474	–	–	**1892**	45.00		

Des: T.Brock

Obverse 1

Des: L.Wyon

Reverse A

No.	Dies[1]		DATE	MINT STATE	3d Dies[2]
1480	**1 A**	Set of 4d, 3d, 2d & 1d	**1893**	38.00	1 A
1481	–	–	**1894**	36.00	
1482	–	–	**1895**	36.00	
1483	–	–	**1896**	36.00	
1484	–	–	**1897**	36.00	
1485	–	–	**1898**	36.00	
1486	–	–	**1899**	36.00	
1487	–	–	**1900**	36.00	
1488	–	–	**1901**	36.00	

1: These coins generally have proof-like surfaces & are plain edged.

2: These dies, where noted, are from the threepence series.

EDWARD VII

9th November 1841 – 6th May 1910

CROWNS

Des: G.W.DeSaulles

Obverse 1

Des: B.Pistrucci

Reverse A

No.	Dies	Raised EDGE YEAR	DATE	MINT STATE	M MATT PROOF
1500	**1 A**	**II**	**1902**	115.00	130.00

Note: All edges are read with obv. uppermost. Edge year varies in width.

HALFCROWNS

Des: G.DeSaulles

Obverse 1

Des: G.DeSaulles

Reverse A

No.	Dies	DATE	MINT STATE	M MATT PROOF
1510	**1 A** [1]	**1902**	45.00	55.00
1511	–	**1903**	480.00	
1512	–	**1904**	270.00	
1513	–	**1905**	900.00	
1514	–	**1906**	120.00	
1515	–	**1907**	120.00	
1516	–	**1908**	140.00	
1517	–	**1909**	110.00	
1518	–	**1910**	70.00	

1: Both obv. & rev. for 1902 have raised edge rims with small designs, probably in anticipation of border beads.

Note: From 1903 onwards designs were pantographically enlarged producing no varieties.

FLORINS

Des: DeSaulles

Obverse 1

Des: DeSaulles

Reverse type

Rev. A
'S' of 'Shilling' lower than 'hill'. Narrow 'N' in 'rin'.

Rev. C
Wide tilted 'N' in 'rin'. Right leg of 'N' higher.

Rev. B
'S' of 'Shilling' level with 'hill'. 'Rin' in line.

No.	Dies	DATE	MINT STATE	M MATT PROOF
1530	**1 A** [1]	**1902**	40.00	38.00
1531	**1 B**	**1903**	70.00	
1532	**1 C**	**1904**	115.00	
1533	–	**1905**	200.00	
1534	–	**1906**	80.00	
1535	–	**1907**	85.00	
1536	–	**1908**	100.00	
1537	–	**1909**	105.00	
1538	–	**1910**	55.00	

1: Both obv. & rev. designs enlarge towards 1910, producing no die varieties. 1907 – 1910 are the largest & have slight indentations to letter bases. 1910 coins have R.H. legend slightly nearer border.

SHILLINGS

Des: DeSaulles

Obverse type

Des: DeSaulles

Reverse A

Obv. 1
'E' of 'Dei' has long upper arm.

Obv. 2
'E' of 'Dei' has short upper arm.

No.	Dies	DATE	MINT STATE	M MATT PROOF
1550	1 A [1]	1902	18.00	24.00
1551	–	1903	52.00	
1552	–	1904	75.00	
1553	2 A	–	55.00	
1554	1 A	1905	*	
1555	2 A	–	400.00	
1556	1 A	1906	65.00	
1557	2 A	–	28.00	
1558	–	1907	38.00	
1559	–	1908	70.00	
1560	–	1909	55.00	
1561	–	1910	22.00	

1: Rev. designs enlarge towards 1910, but produce no die varieties. 1907 has the largest rev. design & 1902 the smallest.

SIXPENCES

Des: DeSaulles

Obverse 1

Des: L.C.Wyon

Reverse A

No.	Dies	DATE	MINT STATE	M MATT PROOF
1570	1 A	1902	14.00	15.00
1571	–	1903	28.00	
1572	– [1]	1904	50.00	
1573	– [1]	1905	38.00	
1574	–	1906	22.00	
1575	–	1907	22.00	
1576	–	1908	38.00	
1577	–	1909	28.00	
1578	–	1910	15.00	

1: Reverses for 1904 & 1905 are from retouched dies having thicker foliage.

THREEPENCES

Des: DeSaulles

Obv. type

Des: L.Wyon

Rev. type

Obv. 1
'Ind: Imp:' spaced. 'I' of 'Britt' to space.

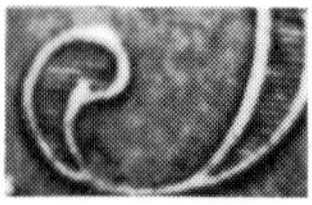

Rev. A
'3' with small ball. '3' has long neck.

Obv. 2
'Ind: Imp:' close. 'I' of 'Britt' to bead.

Rev. B
'3' with large ball. '3' has short neck.

No.	Dies[1]	DATE	MINT STATE
1590	**1 A**	**1902**	6.00
1591	–	**1903**	12.00
1592	–	**1904**	35.00
1593	**1 B**	–	40.00
1594	**2 A**	–	80.00
1595	**2 B**	–	32.00
1596	**1 B**	**1905**	*
1597	**2 B**	–	28.00
1598	**1 B**	**1906**	20.00
1599	**2 B**	–	28.00
1600	**1 B**	**1907**	11.00
1601	–	**1908**	11.00
1602	–	**1909**	12.00
1603	–	**1910**	10.00

1: These coins are plain edged.

MAUNDY SETS

Des: DeSaulles

Obverse 1

Des: L.Wyon

Reverse A

No.	Dies[1]		DATE	MINT STATE	M MATT PROOF P.Edge	3d Dies[2]
1610	**1 A**	Set of 4d, 3d, 2d & 1d	**1902**	40.00	40.00	
1611	–	–	**1903**	38.00		
1612	–	–	**1904**	38.00		
1613	–	–	**1905**	38.00		
1614	–	–	**1906**	38.00		
1615	–	–	**1907**	38.00		
1616	–	–	**1908**	38.00		
1617	–	–	**1909**	48.00		
1618	–	–	**1910**	55.00		

1: These coins generally have proof-like surfaces & are plain edged.
2: These dies, when noted, are from the threepence series.

GEORGE V

3rd June 1865 – 20th January 1936

CROWNS

Des: B.McKennal

Obverse 1

Des: Kruger Gray

Reverse type

Rev. A
'D' of 'Def' to bead.

Rev. B
'D' of 'Def' to space.

No.	Dies	DATE	MINT STATE .500	P PROOF	M MATT PROOF
1630	**1 A**	**1927**		140.00	290.00
1631	**1 B**	**1928**	150.00	*	
1632	–	**1929**	180.00	450.00	
1633	–	**1930**	185.00	450.00	
1634	–	**1931**	200.00	470.00	
1635	–	**1932**	270.00	900.00	
1636	–	**1933**	160.00	450.00	
1637	–	**1934**	£1150	£2000	
1638	–	**1936**	260.00	£1000	

Des: B.McKennal

Obverse 1

Des: P.Metcalf

Reverse type

Rev. A
Sword point to bead.

Rev. B
Sword point to space.

Note: Edges are read either obv. or rev. uppermost. Rev. B illustration is simulated.

No.	Dies		Incuse EDGE YEAR	DATE	MINT STATE	K PROOF LIKE[1]	P PROOF[2]	PP PROOF Raised EDGE[3]	G GOLD Raised EDGE
1650	**1 A**		**XXV**	**1935**	11.00	26.00	*		
1651	–		–	–				225.00	£7000
1652	–	Error edge [4]	–	–	400.00				
1653	–	– [5]	–	–				£1000	
1654	**1 B**		–	–	*		£1000		

1: A 'Specimen' piece superior to currency issue.
2: Thin edge lettering in places. Some may occur in sterling silver – examine 'ring', low note sterling, higher note debased.
3: Sterling (.925) silver.
4: Reads: '– men. Anno – Regni XXV'.
5: Reads: 'Anno Regni et Tutamen '.

Pattern

No.	Designer	OBV.	REV.	Raised EDGE YEAR	DATE	P PROOF
1655	McKennal	'Jubilee' head,	K.Gray's 'St. George'	**XXV**	**1935**	£8500

HALFCROWNS

Des: B.McKennal

Obverse type

Des: G.DeSaulles

Reverse type

Obv. 1
Small head in high relief. Close spaced 'Rex'.

Obv. 2
Medium head, 24½mm & away from 'A: B'. Wide spaced 'Rex'.

Obv. 3
Large head, 25mm. Low relief. Wide spaced 'Rex'.

Obv. 4
'Modified effigy'. Initials to rear of truncation.

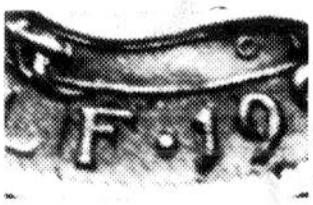

Rev. A
Raised garter edge above 'F . 19'. Colon of 'Def' points to pearl.

Rev. B
Small design. Plain edge above 'F . 19' forming a pocket above 'C'.

Rev. C
Plain garter edge above 'F . 19'. Colon of 'Def' points to pearl.

Rev. D
Legend close to garter. Colon of 'Def' points to space.

Note: Small enlargements or reductions of design occurs, generally for one specific year & are noted only where die varieties are produced or distinctly noticeable.

No.	Dies		DATE	MINT STATE .925	MINT .500 DULL[1]	MINT .500 Bright	P PROOF
1660	**1 A**		**1911**	60.00			100.00
1661	–	Chamfered rim	–				80.00
1662	–		**1912**	85.00			
1663	–		**1913**	90.00			
1664	–		**1914**	22.00			
1665	–		**1915**	18.00			
1666	–		**1916**	18.00			
1667	–		**1917**	26.00			
1668	–		**1918**	18.00			
1669	–	Smaller rev. design[2]	–	45.00			
1670	–		**1919**	28.00			
1671	–	Smaller rev. design[3]	–	50.00			
1672	–		**1920**		40.00		
1673	**1 B**[4]		–		90.00		
1674	**2 A**		–		200.00		
1675	**3 A**		–		40.00		
1676	**3 B**		–		100.00		
1677	–[6]		**1921**		90.00		
1678	**3 C**		–		40.00		
1679	–	Larger rev. design[5]	–		70.00		
1680	–		**1922**		65.00		
1681	**3 D**		–		95.00		
1682	**3 C**		–			75.00	
1683	**3 D**		–			50.00	
1684	–		**1923**			22.00	
1685	–		**1924**			55.00	
1686	–		**1925**			220.00	
1687	–	Chamfered rim	–			260.00	
1688	–		**1926**			60.00	
1689	–	No stops after 'Omn'[7]	–			95.00	
1690	**4 D**		–			85.00	*
1691	–		**1927**			23.00	*

1. This 'dull' alloy – being either 40% copper & 10% nickel (from old shell casings) or 45% copper & 5% manganese – readily tones to a darkish grey.
The 'bright' alloy being 50% copper & heavily 'blanched', retains its much whiter appearance due to the slightly higher surface fineness.
2: This rev. has thick rims almost matching its obv. with the second '1' & '8' both centred over a space & with second '1' closer to garter buckle. This rare rev. also exists with a wider spaced '18'.
3: This rev. has shorter '1's in date with '9's more upright.
4: This rev. (for obv. 1) has a pronounced die crack on the right hand outer part of garter by the 3 o'clock stop.
5: This rev. (the largest for 1921) has the 'O' in 'Honi' evenly shaped instead of thinning towards the base.
6: Rev. B for 1921 has second '1' in date pointing to space not a bead as usual.
7: These filled-in dies also occur: no upper stop; no lower stop; no colon after 'Gra'.

Des: B.McKennal

Obverse type

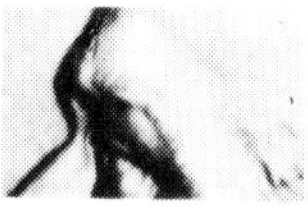

Obv. 1
Shallow forehead & centre part indented. Prominent eyebrow.

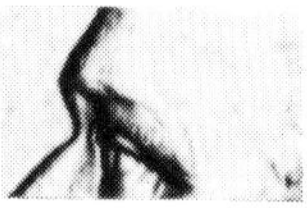

Obv. 2
'Modified' head die, 'full' forehead & shallow eyebrow.

Rev. F
'D' of 'Fid' to space.
'D' of 'Def' to bead.
'E' of 'Def' to space.

Rev. G
'D' of 'Fid' to bead.
'D' of 'Def' l. of bead.
'E' of 'Def' r. of bead.

Rev. H
'D' of 'Fid' to space.
'D' of 'Def' r. of bead.
'E' of 'Def' to space.

Des: Kruger Gray

Reverse type

Rev. A
'D' of 'Fid' l. of bead.
'D' of 'Def' to space.
'E' of 'Def' to bead.

Rev. B
'D' of 'Fid' to space.
'D' of 'Def' to bead.
'E' of 'Def' l. of bead.

Rev. C
'D' of 'Fid' r. of bead.
'D' of 'Def' r. of bead.
'E' of 'Def' l. of bead.

Rev. D
'D' of 'Fid' to space.
'D' of 'Def' to space.
'E' of 'Def' l. of bead.

Rev. E
'D' of 'Fid' to bead.
'D' of 'Def' to space.
'E' of 'Def' r. of bead.

No.	Dies		DATE	MINT STATE	P PROOF	M MATT PROOF
1700	**1 A**		**1927**		33.00	70.00
1701	**1 B**		**1928**	10.00	*	
1702	**2 B** [1]		—	45.00	*	
1703	**1 C**		—	18.00	*	
1704	**1 D**		**1929**	11.00	*	
1705	**1 E**		—	14.00	360.00	
1706	—		**1930**	145.00	750.00	
1707	—		**1931**	13.00	350.00	
1708	—		**1932**	28.00	400.00	
1709	—		**1933**	14.00	*	
1710	—	Larger rev. design (28½mm)	—	17.00	350.00	
1711	**1 F**		**1934**	42.00	460.00	
1712	**1 G**		**1935**	13.00	350.00	
1713	**1 H**		**1936**	9.00	330.00	

1: This obv. uses the 1926 'modified' head puncheon & has a thick obv. rim. The high relief is detected by placing the coin head-down on a level surface — the coin will rock.

FLORINS

Des: McKennal

Obverse type

Des: L.C.Wyon

Reverse type

Obv. 1
'I' of 'Georgivs' to bead. 'Shallow' neck.

Obv. 2
'I' of 'Georgivs' to space. 'Full' neck.

Obv. 3
'I' of 'Georgivs' l. of bead. Large low relief head.

Rev. F
Small design. 'N' away from shield. 'L' points to space.

Rev. G
Legend nearer beads. Left leg of 'N' to space.

Rev. A
Small design. No lines under crown arches. Thick rims.

Rev. B
Large design. Lines under crown arches. Thin rims.

Rev. C
Line under l. arches. 'N' midway from shield. 'L' points to space.

Rev. D
Small design. Thick rim. 'N' away from shield. 'L' points to space.

Rev. E
Small design. 'N' close to shield. 'L' points to bead.

No.	Dies		DATE	MINT STATE .925	P PROOF
1730	**1 A**		**1911**	55.00	80.00
1731	**2 A**		–	35.00	60.00
1732	**2 B**		**1912**	45.00	
1733	**2 C**		**1913**	65.00	
1734	–	Smaller rev. design [1]	–	90.00	
1735	–		**1914**	27.00	
1736	**2 D**		–	30.00	
1737	**2 E**	'1' of '14' right of bead	–	17.00	
1738	–		**1915**	22.00	
1739	–		**1916**	17.00	
1740	–		**1917**	28.00	
1741	–		**1918**	16.00	
1742	–	Smaller rev. design [2]	–	90.00	
1743	–		**1919**	28.00	

1: 2nd. '1' in date points to space, not right of bead as usual. Also known wide '13'.
2: Has thick rim (matching obv.) & close date with '8' central to space (usual l. of bead).

No.	Dies		DATE	MINT .500 DULL	MINT .500 Bright
1744	**2 E**		**1920**	42.00	
1745	–	Smaller rev. design[1]	–	60.00	
1746	**3 E**		–	37.00	
1747	**3 F**		**1921**	35.00	
1748	**3 E**		**1922**	35.00	
1749	–		–		40.00
1750	–	Smaller rev. design[2]	–		60.00
1751	–		**1923**		28.00
1752	**2 E**		–		120.00
1753	**3 E**		**1924**		50.00
1754	**3 G**		**1925**		160.00
1755	–		**1926**		60.00

1: Slightly longer beads at top with '0' in date 'hand-struck' & centred over space.
2: Has thick rim with both '2's in date 'hand-struck' & are mis-aligned. They are closer together & the second '2' tilts nearer the border beads.

Des: McKennal

Obverse 1

Des: K.Gray

Reverse type

Rev. A Top cross to space.

Rev. C Top cross to bead.

Rev. B Top cross left of bead.

No.	Dies	DATE	MINT STATE	P PROOF	M MATT PROOF
1770	**1 A**	**1927**		45.00	85.00
1771	–	**1928**	14.00	*	
1772	–	**1929**	14.00	300.00	
1773	–	**1930**	26.00	350.00	
1774	–	**1931**	18.00	320.00	
1775	–	**1932**	125.00	700.00	
1776	–	**1933**	16.00	330.00	
1777	**1 B**	**1935**	14.00	280.00	
1778	**1 C**	**1936**	7.00	260.00	

SHILLINGS

Des: McKennal Des: DeSaulles

Obverse type

Reverse type

Obv. 1
'I' of 'Georgivs' to space.
'Shallow' neck.

Obv. 2
'I' of 'Georgivs' to bead.
'Shallow' neck.

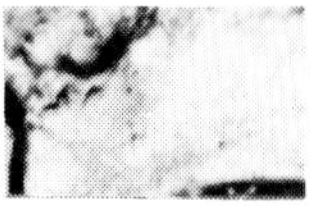

Obv. 3
'I' of 'Georgivs' to bead.
'Full' neck.

Obv. 4
'I' of 'Georgivs' to space.
Low relief head.

Obv. 5
'I' of 'Georgivs' to bead.
Low relief head.

Obv. 6
'I' of 'Georgivs' to space.
'Modified effigy'.

Rev. A
Small letters, close together, esp. 'M' & 'P'.

Rev. B
'D' of 'Ind' r. of bead.
Right leg of 'N' in 'Ind' to space.

Rev. C
'D' of 'Ind' left of bead & more aligned.

Rev. D
Tuft between 'I' & 'M'.
Right leg of 'N' in 'Ind' to bead.

Rev. E
Tuft close to 'M'.
Right leg of 'N' in 'Ind' to space.

Rev. F
Tuft between 'I' & 'M'.
Right leg of 'N' in 'Ind' to bead.

P

No.	Dies		DATE	MINT STATE .925	PROOF
1790	**1 A**		**1911**	16.00	*
1791	**2 A**		–	12.00	*
1792	**3 A**		–	18.00	45.00
1793	–	Chamfered rim	–		35.00
1794	–		**1912**	28.00	
1795	**3 B**		–	17.00	
1796	–		**1913**	55.00	
1797	–		**1914**	11.00	
1798	–		**1915**	9.00	
1799	–		**1916**	10.00	
1800	–		**1917**	16.00	
1801	–		**1918**	15.00	
1802	**3 C**		**1919**	22.00	

No.	Dies		DATE	MINT .500 DULL	MINT .500 Bright	O MINT OVER .500 [1]	N NICKEL
1803	**3 B**		**1920**	22.00			
1804	**4 B**		–	32.00			
1805	**3 D**		**1921**	85.00		120.00	
1806	**4 D**		–	42.00			
1807	**4 E**		–	75.00			
1808	**5 D**		–	60.00			
1809	**5 E**		–	30.00			
1810	–		**1922**	27.00			
1811	–	Larger rev. design (22mm)	–	45.00			
1812	–		–		38.00		
1813	–	Larger rev. design (22mm)	–		*		
1814	–		**1923**		22.00		280.00
1815	–		**1924**		30.00		250.00
1816	–	Metric flan [2]	–				350.00
1817	**5 F**		**1925**		50.00		
1818	–	Chamfered rim	–		60.00		
1819	–		**1926**		22.00		
1820	**6 F**		–		16.00		
1821	–		**1927**		22.00		

1: Inadvertent issue, examine 'ring' – higher the fineness, lower the note produced.
2: Weighs 5 grms (87% normal).

Des: McKennal

Obverse 1

Des: K.Gray

Reverse type

Rev. C
'I' of 'Ind' to space.
r. leg of 'H' to bead.
'D' of 'Def' to bead.

Rev. A
'I' of 'Ind' to bead.
r. leg of 'H' to space.
'D' of 'Def' to space.

Rev. D
'I' of 'Ind' to space.
r. leg of 'H' to bead.
'D' of 'Def' to space.

Rev. B
'I' of 'Ind' to space.
r. leg of 'H' to space.
'D' of 'Def' to space.

No.	Dies	DATE	MINT STATE	P PROOF	M MATT PROOF	N NICKEL
1830	**1 A**	**1925**				£1400 [1]
1831	–	**1927**	25.00	22.00	42.00	
1832	–	**1928**	7.00	*		
1833	–	**1929**	8.00	100.00		
1834	–	**1930**	32.00	230.00		

1: This rev. has designer's initials together instead of separated by part of tail.

No.	Dies	DATE	MINT STATE	P PROOF
1835	**1 A**	**1931**	18.00	125.00
1836	–	**1932**	14.00	110.00
1837	–	**1933**	10.00	120.00
1838	**1 B**	**1934**	28.00	170.00
1839	**1 C**	**1935**	7.00	100.00
1840	**1 D**	**1936**	6.00	90.00

SIXPENCES

Des: McKennal

Obverse type

Des: DeSaulles

Reverse type

Obv. 1
'I' of 'Britt' to bead. 'Shallow' neck.

Obv. 2
'I' of 'Britt' to space. 'Full' neck.

Obv. 3
'I' of 'Dei' to space. Broad rim.

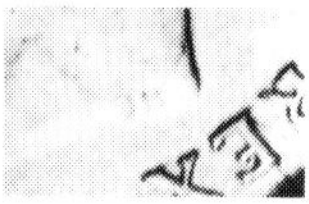

Obv. 4
'I' of 'Dei' to bead. 'Modified effigy'.

Rev. A
Colon of 'Fid' to bead. Small design. Lion has small face.

Rev. B
Colon of 'Fid' to space. Lion has broad face & less mane.

Rev. C
Colon of 'Fid' left of bead. Broad rim.

No.	Dies	DATE	MINT STATE .925	P PROOF
1860	**1 A**	**1911**	90.00	
1861	**1 B**	–	*	
1862	**2 A**	–	55.00	
1863	**2 B**	–	11.00	28.00
1864	–	**1912**	20.00	
1865	–	**1913**	25.00	
1866	–	**1914**	10.00	
1867	–	**1915**	12.00	
1868	–	**1916**	10.00	
1869	–	**1917**	27.00	
1870	–	**1918**	11.00	
1871	–	**1919**	13.00	
1872	–	**1920**	28.00	

No.	Dies	DATE	MINT .500 DULL [1]	MINT .500 Bright
1873	**2 B**	**1920**	20.00	
1874	–	**1921**	18.00	
1875	–	**1922**	22.00	
1876	–	–		32.00
1877	–	**1923**		34.00
1878	–	**1924**		18.00
1879	–	**1925**		24.00
1880	**3 C**	–		18.00
1881	–	**1926**		24.00
1882	**4 C**	–		17.00
1883	–	**1927**		18.00

1: These debased 1920 coins are distinguished from sterling issues by examining their 'ring' by placing the coin on finger-tip & gently tap with a pencil. A low note indicates sterling silver & a higher one debased silver.

*: to be confirmed.

Des: McKennal

Obverse type

Des: K.Gray

Reverse type

Obv. 1
Colon after 'Omn:' to bead.
Full titles.

Obv. 2
Colon after 'Omn:' to space.
Full titles.

Rev. A
Left acorn r. of bead.
l. leg of 'A' to bead.
Right acorn l. of bead.

Rev. B
Left acorn l. of bead.
l. leg of 'A' to space.
Right acorn l. of bead.

Rev. C
Left acorn to space.
l. leg of 'A' to bead.
Right acorn to space.

Rev. F
Left acorn to bead.
l. leg of 'A' to bead.
Right acorn to space.

Rev. D
Left acorn to bead.
l. leg of 'A' to bead.
Right acorn to bead.

Rev. G
Left acorn to bead.
l. leg of 'A' to space.
Right acorn to bead.

Rev. E
Left acorn to bead.
l. leg of 'A' to space.
Right acorn to space.

No.	Dies		DATE	MINT STATE	P PROOF	M MATT PROOF	N NICKEL
1890	**4 A** [1]		**1925**				900.00
1891	**1 A**		**1927**		15.00	35.00	
1892	**1 B**		**1928**	5.00	*		
1893	**1 C**		**1929**	6.00	70.00		
1894	**2 D**		**1930**	8.00	80.00		
1895	– [2]		**1931**	6.00	75.00		
1896	–		**1932**	12.00	90.00		
1897	–		**1933**	6.00	75.00		
1898	**2 E**		**1934**	11.00	90.00		
1899	**2 F**		**1935**	6.00	70.00		
1900	–	Smaller rev. design [3]	–	35.00			
1901	**2 G**		**1936**	3.00	65.00		

1: This coin uses obv. '4' from previous issue, omitting 'Fid: Def: Ind: Imp:'.
2: Closer milling hereonwards.
3: This rev. has smaller beads & thinner stems due to weak hubbing.

THREEPENCES

Des: McKennal

Obverse type

Des: L.C.Wyon

Reverse type

Obv. 1
'I' of 'Georgivs' to bead.
'Shallow' neck.

Obv. 2
'I' of 'Georgivs' right of bead.
'Full' neck.

Obv. 3
'I' of 'Georgivs' left of bead.
'P' is mis-aligned.

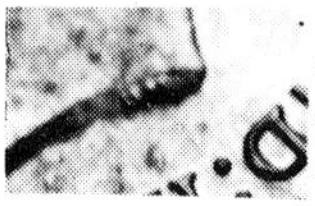

Obv. 4
'I' of 'Georgivs' to space.
'Modified effigy'.

Rev. A
Top left-hand leaf is cone shaped.

Rev. B
Top leaf emanates from left-hand stalk.

Rev. C
Top leaf emanates centrally from berry stalks.

Note: Reverses 'B' & 'C' represent the principal configurations for this top leaf, but they vary slightly from year to year.
These coins are plain edged.

No.	Dies		DATE	MINT STATE .925	MINT .500 DULL	MINT .500 Bright	N NICKEL PLAIN EDGE
1920	**1 A**		**1911**	5.00			
1921	**2 A**		–	6.00			
1922	**1 B**		–	*			
1923	**2 B**		–	24.00			
1924	–		**1912**	6.00			
1925	–		**1913**	6.00			
1926	–		**1914**	12.00			
1927	**3 B**		–	7.00			
1928	–		**1915**	6.00			
1929	–		**1916**	5.00			
1930	–		**1917**	5.00			
1931	**3 C**		**1918**	6.00			
1932	**3 B**		**1919**	5.00			
1933	–	last '9' over '8'	–	30.00			
1934	**3 C** [1]		**1920**	6.00			
1935	– [1]		–		5.00		
1936	**3 B**		**1921**		5.00		
1937	–	small '2'	–		25.00		
1938	–		**1922**		8.00		
1939	–		–			17.00	
1940	–		**1923**				160.00
1941	–		**1925**			20.00	
1942	–		**1926**			32.00	
1943	**4 B**		–			17.00	

1: These coins are distinguished by examining their 'ring' – a low note indicates sterling silver whilst a higher note debased silver.

Des: McKennal

Obverse 1

Des: K.Gray

Reverse A

No.	Dies	DATE	MINT STATE	E PROOF PLAIN EDGE	M MATT PROOF P.Edge	N NICKEL PLAIN EDGE
1950	**1 A**	**1925**				600.00
1951	–	**1927**		42.00	75.00	
1952	–	**1928**	12.00	*		
1953	–	**1930**	9.00	65.00		
1954	–	**1931**	5.00	60.00		
1955	–	**1932**	3.00	55.00		
1956	–	**1933**	3.00	55.00		
1957	–	**1934**	3.00	55.00		
1958	–	**1935**	2.00	50.00		
1959	–	**1936**	2.00	50.00		

*: to be confirmed.

MAUNDY SETS

Des: McKennal

Obverse type

Des: L.C.Wyon

Reverse type

Obv. 1
High relief head.
'B.M.' about centre of truncation.

Obv. 2
Low relief head.
'Modified effigy',
'B.M.' at rear end.

Rev. A
Large centre pearls. Thick irregular foliage.

Rev. B
Small centre pearls. Thin symmetrical foliage.

No.	Dies [1]		DATE	MINT STATE .925	MINT .500 DULL	MINT .500 Bright	E PROOF PLAIN EDGE	3d Dies [2]
1970	**1 A**	Set of 4d, 3d, 2d & 1d	**1911**	45.00			45.00	
1971	–	–	**1912**	42.00				
1972	–	–	**1913**	42.00				
1973	–	–	**1914**	47.00				
1974	–	–	**1915**	40.00				
1975	–	–	**1916**	42.00				
1976	–	–	**1917**	40.00				
1977	–	–	**1918**	40.00				
1978	–	–	**1919**	40.00				
1979	–	–	**1920**	40.00				3 C
1980	–	–	**1921**		42.00			3 B
1981	–	–	**1922**		42.00			–
1982	–	–	**1923**			47.00		–
1983	–	–	**1924**			47.00		–
1984	–	–	**1925**			45.00		–
1985	–	–	**1926**			45.00		–
1986	–	–	**1927**			42.00		–
1987	**2 A**	–	**1928**			45.00		4 B
1988	–	–	**1929**			47.00		–
1989	**2 B**	–	**1930**			42.00		
1990	–	–	**1931**			42.00		
1991	–	–	**1932**			42.00		
1992	–	–	**1933**			42.00		
1993	–	–	**1934**			42.00		
1994	–	–	**1935**			50.00		
1995	–	–	**1936**			55.00		

1: These coins have proof-like surfaces & are plain edged.
2: These dies, where noted, are from the threepence series.

EDWARD VIII

23rd June 1894 – 28th May 1972

CROWN

Pattern

No.	Designer	OBV.	REV.	DATE	P PROOF
2000	H.Paget	Bare head,	K.Gray's *Royal arms*	1937	£50000

HALFCROWN

Pattern

No.	Designer	OBV.	REV.	DATE	P PROOF
2001	H.Paget	Bare head,	K.Gray's *Royal Standard*	1937	£20000

FLORIN

Pattern

No.	Designer	OBV.	REV.	DATE	P PROOF
2002	H.Paget	Bare head,	K.Gray's *Crowned Rose*	1937	£12000

SHILLING

Pattern

No.	Designer	OBV.	REV.	DATE	P PROOF
2003	H.Paget	Bare head,	K.Gray's *Scottish* type	1937	£10000

SIXPENCE

Pattern

No.	Designer	OBV.	REV.	DATE	P PROOF
2004	H.Paget	Bare head,	K.Gray's *Interlinked Rings*	1937	£7500

THREEPENCE

Pattern

No.	Designer	OBV.	REV.	DATE	P PROOF
2005	H.Paget	Bare head,	K.Gray's *Interlinked Rings*	1937	£3500

Note: The crown, florin & shilling are those employed for George VI's coinage but with a 'G' substituted on the florin.
These coins are struck in .500 fine silver.

GEORGE VI

14th December 1895 – 6th February 1952

CROWNS

Des: H.Paget

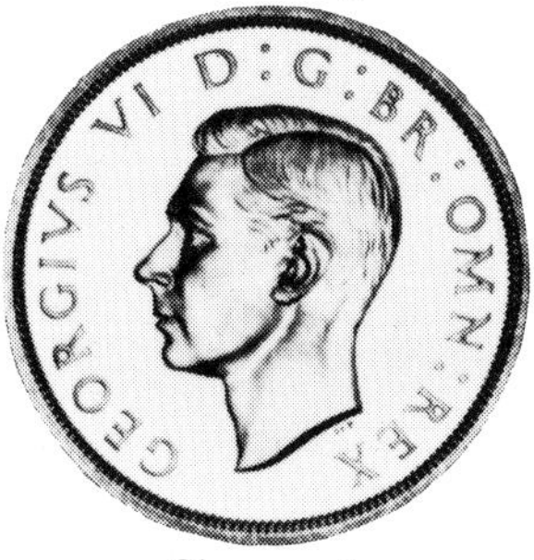

Obverse 1

Des: K.Gray

Reverse A

No.	Dies	DATE	MINT STATE	P PROOF	V V.I.P. PROOF[1]	M MATT PROOF
2010	**1 A**	**1937**	15.00	38.00	350.00	75.00

1: V.I.P. strikings have 'frosting' on designs. This piece may occur in sterling silver.

Des: H.Paget

Obverse 1

Des: Pistrucci

Reverse A

No.	Dies	Incuse EDGE YEAR[1]	DATE	P PROOF	E PROOF PLAIN EDGE[2]	V V.I.P. PROOF[3]
2020	**1 A**	**MCMLI**	**1951**	5.00	600.00	300.00

1: Reads: '*MDCCLI Civium Industria Floret Civitas MCMLI' – obv. or rev. uppermost.
2: Unintentional strikings from unedged blanks.
3: 'V.I.P.' strikings have 'frosting' on designs.

DOUBLEFLORINS

Patterns

No.	Designer	OBV.	REV.	DATE	P PROOF
2021	H.Paget	Bare head,	Pistrucci's Gartered St. George	**1950**	£3200
2022	–	– edge stamped 'four shillings'	–	–	£3300

HALFCROWNS

Des: H.Paget

Obverse 1

Des: K.Gray

Reverse A

No.	Dies	DATE	MINT STATE .500	MINT CUPRO NICKEL	P PROOF .500	P PROOF CUPRO NICKEL
2030	**1 A**	**1937**	7.00		10.00	
2031	–	**1938**	18.00		280.00	
2032	–	**1939**	6.00		250.00	
2033	–	**1940**	6.00		250.00	
2034	–	**1941**	5.00		250.00	
2035	–	**1942**	4.00		250.00	
2036	–	**1943**	6.00		250.00	
2037	–	**1944**	4.00		250.00	
2038	–	**1945**	3.00		230.00	
2039	–	**1946**	3.00		230.00	
2040	–	–		*		380.00
2041	–	**1947**		4.00		230.00
2042	–	**1948**		3.00		230.00

Des: H.Paget

Obverse 1

Des: K.Gray

Reverse A

No.	Dies	DATE	MINT STATE	P PROOF
2060	**1 A**	**1949**	5.00	230.00
2061	–	**1950**	7.00	10.00
2062	–	**1951**	9.00	8.00
2063	–	**1952**	£8500 [1]	*

1: Price for V.F. condition. Does not exist mint in private hands.

Note: As with other 20th century coins, enlargement or reduction of design occurs generally for a specific year. With this reign reverses enlarge during the debased series.

FLORINS

Des: H.Paget — Des: K.Gray

Obverse 1

Reverse type

Rev. A 'D' of 'Ind' to bead.

Rev. B 'D' of 'Ind' to space.

No.	Dies	DATE	MINT STATE .500	MINT CUPRO NICKEL	P PROOF .500	P PROOF CUPRO NICKEL
2070	**1 A**	**1937**	5.00		9.00	
2071	**1 B**	–	12.00		*	
2072	–	**1938**	16.00		220.00	
2073	–	**1939**	4.50		180.00	
2074	–	**1940**	5.00		180.00	
2075	–	**1941**	5.00		180.00	
2076	–	**1942**	3.00		180.00	
2077	–	**1943**	4.00		180.00	
2078	–	**1944**	4.00		180.00	
2079	–	**1945**	3.00		170.00	
2080	–	**1946**	3.00		170.00	
2081	–	–		*		300.00
2082	–	**1947**		3.00		170.00
2083	–	**1948**		2.50		170.00

Des: H.Paget — Des: K.Gray

Obverse 1

Reverse type

Rev. A 'F' of 'Def' to bead.

Rev. B 'F' of 'Def' to space.

No.	Dies	DATE	MINT STATE	P PROOF
2100	**1 A**	**1949**	8.00	170.00
2101	–	**1950**	8.00	6.00
2102	**1 B**	**1951**	9.00	6.00

SHILLINGS

Des: H.Paget

Obverse 1

Des: K.Gray

'English' type

Rev. A
'I' of 'Ind' to space.

Rev. B
'I' of 'Ind' to bead.

No.	Dies		DATE	MINT STATE .500	MINT CUPRO NICKEL	P PROOF .500	P PROOF CUPRO NICKEL
2110	**1 A**		**1937**	6.00		7.00	
2111	–		**1938**	22.00		150.00	
2112	–		**1939**	4.50		120.00	
2113	–		**1940**	5.00		120.00	
2114	–		**1941**	5.00		120.00	
2115	–		**1942**	3.50		120.00	
2116	–		**1943**	3.00		120.00	
2117	–	Die axis inverted [1]	–	45.00			
2118	–		**1944**	3.00		110.00	
2119	–		**1945**	2.50		110.00	
2120	–		**1946**	2.50		*	
2121	**1 B**		–	6.00		110.00	
2122	–		–		*		160.00
2123	–		**1947**		6.00		110.00
2124	–		**1948**		3.00		110.00

1: Unintentional striking.

Des: H.Paget

Obverse 1

Des: K.Gray

Reverse **A**

No.	Dies	DATE	MINT STATE	P PROOF
2140	**1 A**	**1949**	6.00	110.00
2141	–	**1950**	6.00	5.00
2142	–	**1951**	6.50	5.00
2143	–	**1952**		£5000

Des: H.Paget

Obverse 1

Des: K.Gray

'Scottish' type

No.	Dies	DATE	MINT STATE .500	MINT CUPRO NICKEL	P PROOF .500	P PROOF CUPRO NICKEL
2150	**1 A**	**1937**	4.50		6.00	
2151	–	**1938**	20.00		150.00	
2152	–	**1939**	5.00		120.00	
2153	–	**1940**	5.50		120.00	
2154	–	**1941**	6.00		120.00	
2155	–	**1942**	6.00		120.00	
2156	–	**1943**	5.00		120.00	
2157	–	**1944**	5.50		110.00	
2158	–	**1945**	2.50		110.00	
2159	–	**1946**	2.50		110.00	
2160	–	–		*		*
2161	–	**1947**		4.00		110.00
2162	–	**1948**		3.00		110.00

Des: H.Paget

Obverse 1

Des: K.Gray

Reverse A

No.	Dies	DATE	MINT STATE	P PROOF
2180	**1 A**	**1949**	7.00	110.00
2181	–	**1950**	6.00	5.00
2182	–	**1951**	6.00	5.00
2183	–	**1952**		*

SIXPENCES

Des: H.Paget

Obverse 1

Des: K.Gray

Reverse type

Rev. A 'I' of 'Fid' to bead.

Rev. B 'I' of 'Fid' to space.

No.	Dies	DATE	MINT STATE .500	MINT CUPRO NICKEL	P PROOF .500	P PROOF CUPRO NICKEL
2190	**1 A**	**1937**	3.00		4.00	
2191	–	**1938**	7.00		75.00	
2192	–	**1939**	4.00		55.00	
2193	–	**1940**	3.50		55.00	
2194	–	**1941**	4.50		55.00	
2195	–	**1942**	2.00		55.00	
2196	**1 B**	**1943**	2.00		55.00	
2197	–	**1944**	1.50		55.00	
2198	–	**1945**	1.00		50.00	
2199	–	**1946**	1.00		50.00	
2200	–	–		*		110.00
2201	–	**1947**		2.00		50.00
2202	–	**1948**		1.00		50.00

Des: H.Paget

Obverse 1

Des: K.Gray

Reverse A

No.	Dies	DATE	MINT STATE	P PROOF
2220	**1 A**	**1949**	3.50	50.00
2221	–	**1950**	3.50	4.50
2222	–	**1951**	3.50	3.50
2223	–	**1952**	35.00	250.00

THREEPENCES

Des: Paget

Obv. 1

Des: Gray

Rev. type

Rev. A 'I' of 'Imp' to bead.

Rev. B 'I' of 'Imp' to space.

No.	Dies	DATE	MINT STATE	E PROOF PLAIN EDGE
2230	**1 A**	**1937**	1.50	4.00
2231	**1 B**	–	*	
2232	–	**1938**	1.50	40.00
2233	–	**1939**	7.00	50.00
2234	–	**1940**	2.00	40.00
2235	–	**1941**	2.00	40.00
2236	–	**1942**	15.00	80.00
2237	–	**1943**	17.00	100.00
2238	–	**1944**	25.00	130.00
2239	–	**1945**	*	950.00

MAUNDY SETS

Des: Paget

Obverse 1

Des: Wyon

Reverse A

No.	Dies[1]		DATE	MINT STATE .500	MINT STATE .925	E PROOF PLAIN EDGE
2250	**1 A**	Set of 4d, 3d, 2d & 1d	**1937**	38.00		38.00
2251	–	–	**1938**	42.00		
2252	–	–	**1939**	42.00		
2253	–	–	**1940**	42.00		
2254	–	–	**1941**	42.00		
2255	–	–	**1942**	42.00		
2256	–	–	**1943**	42.00		
2257	–	–	**1944**	42.00		
2258	–	–	**1945**	42.00		
2259	–	–	**1946**	42.00		
2260	–	–	**1947**		43.00	
2261	–	–	**1948**		43.00	

Des: Paget

Obverse 1

Des: Wyon

Reverse A

No.	Dies[1]		DATE	MINT STATE
2270	**1 A**	Set of 4d, 3d, 2d & 1d	**1949**	43.00
2271	–	–	**1950**	43.00
2272	–	–	**1951**	43.00
2273	–	–	**1952**	53.00

1: These coins have proof-like surfaces. Threepences & Maundy sets are plain edged.

21st April 1926 –

CROWNS

Des: G.Ledward

Obverse type

Des: E.Fuller

Reverse A

Obv. 1 'I' in 'Gratia' to bead.

Obv. 2 'I' in 'Gratia' to space.

No.	Dies	Incuse EDGE 1	DATE	MINT STATE	P PROOF	V V.I.P. PROOF 2	M MATT PROOF
2280	**1 A**	Lettered	**1953**	3.00	16.00	300.00	200.00
2281	**2 A**	–	–	5.00	*	*	*

1: Reads: Faith and Truth I Will Bear Unto You', either obv. or rev. uppermost.

Pattern

No.	Designer	OBV.	REV.	Incuse EDGE	DATE	P PROOF
2282	Ledward	As currency,	Shields with large emblems	Lettered	**1953**	£4500

Des: M.Gillick

Obverse 1

Des: E.Fuller

Reverse A

No.	Dies	DATE	MINT STATE	K PROOF LIKE 1	V V.I.P. PROOF 2	S PROOF .925 3	E PLAIN EDGE 4
2290	**1 A**	**1960**	5.50	13.00	350.00	800.00	250.00

1: Struck from polished dies on ordinary flans.
2: 'V.I.P.' strikings have 'frosting' on designs.
3: Examine 'ring', low note .925 silver.
4: Unintentional strikings.

Des: M.Gillick

Obverse 1

Des: O.Nemon

Reverse type

Rev. A
Thick formed 'C' & 'H'.

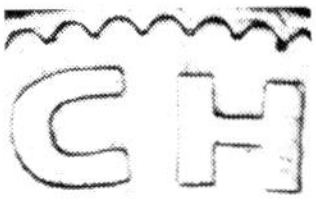

Rev. B
Thin formed 'C' & 'H'.

No.	Dies	DATE	MINT STATE	M SATIN PROOF[1]	E PLAIN EDGE[2]
2300	**1 A**	**1965**	.70		*
2301	**1 B**	–	.70	450.00	20.00

1: This piece has an iridescent surface.
2: Unintentional striking.

HALFCROWNS

Des: M.Gillick

Obverse type

Des: E.Fuller

Reverse A

Obv. 1
'I' of 'Dei' to space.

Obv. 2
'I' of 'Dei' to bead.

No.	Dies	DATE	MINT STATE	P PROOF
2310	**1 A**	**1953**	2.50	*
2311	**2 A**	–	2.50	8.00

Note: Due to the changing status of many overseas possessions, 'Britt Omn' was omitted from all coinage titles after 1953. All currency coins are cupro-nickel. As with earlier 20th century coins, enlargement or reduction of design size occurs generally for a specific year. These are noted where distinctly different.

Des: M.Gillick

Obverse type

Des: E.Fuller

Reverse type

Obv. 1
'I' of 'Gratia' to space.

Obv. 2
'I' of 'Gratia' to bead.

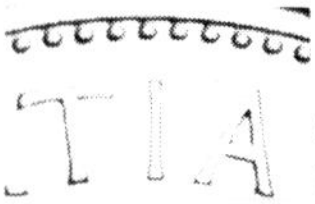

Obv. 3
'I' of 'Gratia' right of bead.

Rev. A
'D' of 'Def' r. of bead. 'E' of 'Def' to bead.

Rev. B
'D' of 'Def' to bead. 'E' of 'Def' to bead.

Rev. C
'D' of 'Def' to space. 'E' of 'Def' r. of bead.

P

No.	Dies		DATE	MINT STATE	PROOF
2320	**1 A**		**1954**	14.00	180.00
2321	**1 B**		**1955**	3.50	170.00
2322	–		**1956**	4.00	180.00
2323	–		**1957**	2.50	170.00
2324	–		**1958**	14.00	200.00
2325	–		**1959**	17.00	230.00
2326	–		**1960**	3.00	170.00
2327	–		**1961**	1.00	150.00
2328	–	Polished flan	–	3.00	
2329	–		**1962**	1.00	
2330	**1 C**		–	4.00	
2331	**2 B**		–	4.00	
2332	**2 C**		–	1.00	160.00
2333	–		**1963**	1.00	160.00
2334	–		**1964**	2.50	
2335	–		**1965**	1.00	
2336	–		**1966**	.50	
2337	–		**1967**	.50	
2338	–		**1970**		*
2339	**3 C**		–		2.50

Note: After 1963 the practice of striking presentation proof sets was discontinued.

FLORINS

Des: M.Gillick

Obverse type

Des: E.Fuller

Reverse A

Obv. 1
'I' of 'Elizabeth' to space.

Obv. 2
'I' of 'Elizabeth' to bead.

P

No.	Dies	DATE	MINT STATE	PROOF
2360	**1 A**	**1953**	1.50	*
2361	**2 A**	—	3.00	5.00

Des: M.Gillick

Obverse type

Des: E.Fuller

Reverse type

Obv. 1
'A' of 'Gratia' to space.

Rev. A
'T' points to bead.

Obv. 2
'A' of 'Gratia' to bead.

Rev. B
'T' points to space.

P

No.	Dies	DATE	MINT STATE	PROOF
2370	**1 A**	**1954**	40.00	240.00
2371	—	**1955**	2.50	125.00
2372	—	**1956**	3.00	125.00
2373	**1 B**	**1957**	30.00	180.00
2374	—	**1958**	14.00	170.00
2375	—	**1959**	35.00	200.00
2376	—	**1960**	2.00	125.00
2377	—	**1961**	2.00	125.00
2378	—	**1962**	1.50	120.00
2379	—	**1963**	1.00	120.00

P

No.	Dies		DATE	MINT STATE	PROOF
2380	**1 B**		**1964**	.50	
2381	–		**1965**	.50	
2382	–		**1966**	.50	
2383	–		**1967**	.40	
2384	–		**1970**		*
2385	**2 B**		–		2.00

SHILLINGS

Des: M.Gillick

Obverse type

Des: W.Gardner

Reverse A

Obv. 1
'I' of 'Elizabeth' to bead.

Obv. 2
'I' of 'Elizabeth' to space.

P

No.	Dies		DATE	MINT STATE	PROOF
2400	**1 A**		**1953**	.50	*
2401	**2 A**		–	1.00	3.00

Des: M.Gillick

Obverse 1

Des: W.Gardner

'English' type

Rev. A
'D' of 'Fid' to bead. 'D' of 'Def' r. of bead.

Rev. C
'D' of 'Fid' to bead. 'D' of 'Def' l. of bead.

Rev. B
'D' of 'Fid' to space. 'D' of 'Def' to bead.

P

No.	Dies		DATE	MINT STATE	PROOF
2410	**1 A**		**1954**	2.00	90.00
2411	**1 B**		**1955**	1.50	80.00
2412	–	Smaller rev. design (19½mm) [1]	–	4.50	*

1: This rev. has a broad rim. Note: Shorter rev. beads from 1957 onwards.

				P
No.	Dies	DATE	MINT STATE	PROOF
2413	**1 B**	**1956**	6.00	*
2414	**1 C**	–	6.00	95.00
2415	–	**1957**	1.00	80.00
2416	–	**1958**	22.00	120.00
2417	–	**1959**	1.00	80.00
2418	–	**1960**	1.00	80.00
2419	–	**1961**	1.00	80.00
2420	–	**1962**	.50	80.00
2421	–	**1963**	.50	80.00
2422	–	**1964**	.50	
2423	–	**1965**	.50	
2424	–	**1966**	.50	
2425	–	**1970**		1.50

Des: M.Gillick

Obverse type

Des: W.Gardner

Reverse A

Obv. 1 'I' of 'Elizabeth' to bead.

Obv. 2 'I' of 'Elizabeth' to space.

				P
No.	Dies	DATE	MINT STATE	PROOF
2440	**1 A**	**1953**	1.00	*
2441	**2 A**	–	1.50	3.00

Des: M.Gillick

Obverse 1

Des: W.Gardner

'Scottish type'

Rev. A 'D' of 'Def' to bead. 'F' of 'Def' to bead.

Rev. C 'D' of 'Def' to space. 'F' of 'Def' l. of bead.

Rev. B 'D' of 'Def' to bead. 'F' of 'Def' to space.

No.	Dies		DATE	MINT STATE	P PROOF
2450	**1 A**		**1954**	1.50	80.00
2451	**1 B**		**1955**	3.50	*
2452	–	Smaller rev. design (19½mm)[1]	–	45.00	*
2453	**1 C**		–	1.50	80.00
2454	–		**1956**	6.00	90.00
2455	–		**1957**	18.00	120.00
2456	–		**1958**	1.00	80.00
2457	–		**1959**	18.00	120.00
2458	–		**1960**	1.00	80.00
2459	–		**1961**	5.50	90.00
2460	–		**1962**	1.00	80.00
2461	–		**1963**	.50	80.00
2462	–		**1964**	.50	
2463	–		**1965**	.50	
2464	–		**1966**	.25	
2465	–		**1970**		1.50

1: This rev. has a broad rim. Note: Shorter rev. beads from 1956 onwards.

SIXPENCES

Des: Gillick

Obv. type

Des: Fuller

Rev. A

Obv. 1
'L' of 'Elizabeth' to bead.

Obv. 2
'L' of 'Elizabeth' to space.

No.	Dies	DATE	MINT STATE	P PROOF
2480	**1 A**	**1953**	1.00	*
2481	**2 A**	–	.50	2.00

Des: Gillick

Obv. type

Des: Fuller

Rev. type

Obv. 1
2nd. 'A' of 'Gratia' to space.

Rev. A
'F' & 'D' of 'Fid' to bead.

Obv. 2
2nd. 'A' of 'Gratia' to bead.

Obv. 3
2nd. 'A' of 'Gratia' to r. of bead.

Rev. B
'F' & 'D' of 'Fid' to space.

Rev. C
'F' & 'D' of 'Fid' to r. of bead.

Rev. D
'F' & 'D' of 'Fid' to l. of bead.

P

No.	Dies	DATE	MINT STATE	PROOF
2490	**1 A**	**1954**	2.50	45.00
2491	--	**1955**	1.00	*
2492	**1 B**	—	1.00	40.00
2493	—	**1956**	1.00	40.00
2494	—	**1957**	.50	40.00
2495	—	**1958**	3.00	45.00
2496	—	**1959**	.25	40.00
2497	—	**1960**	3.00	45.00
2498	—	**1961**	2.50	45.00
2499	—	**1962**	.25	40.00
2500	—	**1963**	.25	40.00
2501	—	**1964**	.25	
2502	**2 B**	—	3.00	
2503	**1 C**	**1965**	9.00	
2504	**2 C**	—	.25	
2505	**2 D**	**1966**	.10	
2506	—	**1967**	.10	
2507	—	**1970**		*
2508	**3 D**	—		1.00

MAUNDY SETS

Des: Gillick

Obverse 1

Des: L.Wyon

Reverse A

No.	Dies[1]		DATE	MINT STATE
2520	**1 A**	Set of 4d, 3d, 2d & 1d	**1953**	220.00

1: These coins have proof-like surfaces & are plain edged.

Des: Gillick

Obverse 1

Des: L.Wyon

Reverse A

No.	Dies[1]		DATE	MINT STATE
2521	**1 A**	Set of 4d, 3d, 2d & 1d	**1954**	48.00
2522	–	–	**1955**	48.00
2523	–	–	**1956**	48.00
2524	–	–	**1957**	48.00
2525	–	–	**1958**	48.00
2526	–	–	**1959**	48.00
2527	–	–	**1960**	48.00
2528	–	–	**1961**	48.00
2529	–	–	**1962**	48.00
2530	–	–	**1963**	48.00
2531	–	–	**1964**	48.00
2532	–	–	**1965**	50.00
2533	–	–	**1966**	50.00
2534	–	–	**1967**	50.00
2535	–	–	**1968**	52.00
2536	–	–	**1969**	52.00
2537	–	–	**1970**	55.00
2538	– [2]	–	**1971**	55.00
2539	–	–	**1972**	55.00
2540	–	–	**1973**	55.00
2541	–	–	**1974**	58.00
2542	–	–	**1975**	60.00
2543	–	–	**1976**	65.00
2544	–	–	**1977**	85.00
2545	–	–	**1978**	70.00
2546	–	–	**1979**	77.00
2547	–	–	**1980**	80.00

1: These coins have proof-like surfaces & are plain edged.

2: Maundy sets dated after 1970 are classified as decimal issues although of identical design.

Proof Sets

Limited strikings from specially prepared dies and blanks imparting a mirror-like finish to the coin field. Unofficial contemporary cases for nineteenth century issues with official standardized cases for twentieth century issues. Many sets are accompanied by gold and copper proofs and these are noted for completeness. Proof sets of other years can be assembled prior to 1927, after which date about a dozen silver and copper sets were struck for official use each year. These listed here constitute the standard issues. Coronation sets were struck for Edward VIII and gold coronation sets for Elizabeth II but neither were issued.

No.	DATE	£5	£2	£1	£½	5s	4s	2/6	2s	E 1s	S 1s	6d	4d	3d	M	B 3d	1d	½d	¼d	½ ¼d	¼ ¼d	F.D.C. SET £
2570	**1826**	L	L	M	M	L		M		M		M					P	P	P			£21500[1]
2571	**1831**		P	P	P	P		P		P		P			P		P	P	P			£14000[1]
2572	**1839**	L		P	P	P		P		P		P	P		P		P	P	P			£24000[1]
2573	**1853**			M	M	L		M	M	M		M	M		P		P	P	P	P	P	£13500[1]
2574	**1887**	M	M	M	M	M	M	M	M	M		M		P								£5800
2575	–					M	M	M	M	M		M		P								680.00
2576	**1893**	M	M	M	M	L		M	M	M		M		P								£6000
2577	–					L		M	M	M		M		P								600.00
2578	**1902**	M	M	M	M	L		M	M	M		M			P							£1950[2]
2579	–			M	M	L		M	M	M		M			P							480.00[2]
2580	**1911**	M	M	M	M			M	M	M		M			P							£3500
2581	–			M	M			M	M	M		M			P							650.00
2582	–							M	M	M		M			P							290.00
2583	**1927**					M		M	M	M		M		P								290.00
2584	**1937**	P	P	P	P																	£2250
2585	–					M		M	M	M	M	M		P	P	D	P	P	P			100.00
2586	**1950**							M	M	M	M	M				D	P	P	P			45.00
2587	**1951**					L		M	M	M	M	M				D	P	P	P			55.00
2588	**1953**					L		M	M	M	M	M				D	P	P	P			38.00
2589	**1970**							M	M	M	M	M				D	P	P				13.00

1: These early sets were privately issued by the Mint's engravers. Proof coins being non-legal tender.
2: The proofs of 1902 were subsequently acid treated imparting a matt surface.

B: Nickel brass, E: English, M: Maundy set, S: Scottish.
D: Dodecagonal edge, L: Lettered edge, M: Milled edge, P: Plain edge.

Decimal Issues

of

Llantrisant

1968 - 1980

TWENTY FIVE PENCES

Des: A.Machin

Obverse 1

Des: A.Machin

Reverse A

No.	Dies	DATE	MINT STATE	P PROOF	S PROOF .925
2600	**1 A**	**1972**	.70	3.00	22.00

Des: A.Machin

Obverse 1

Des: A.Machin

Reverse A

No.	Dies	DATE	MINT STATE	K PROOF LIKE	P PROOF	S PROOF .925
2610	**1 A**	**1977**	.50	1.50	2.50	16.00

Des: A.Machin

Obverse 1

Des: R.Guyatt

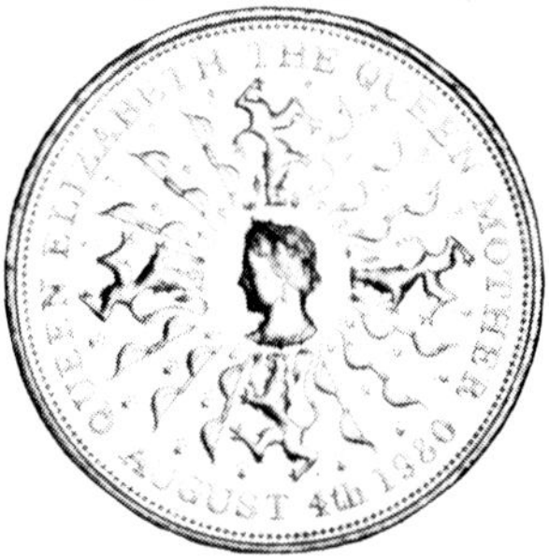

Reverse A

No.	Dies	DATE	MINT STATE	S PROOF .925
2620	**1 A**	**1980**	.35	25.00

FIFTY PENCES

Des: A.Machin

Obverse type

Des: C.Ironside

Reverse type

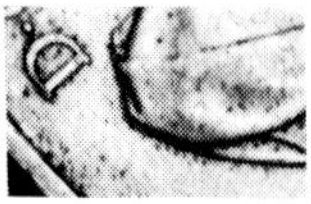

Obv. 1
Small design. Defined head with no base line.

Rev. A
Large legend & Britannia. Legend close to border.

Obv. 2
Large design. Less defined head with base line.

Rev. B
Small legend & Britannia. Legend away from border.

Obv. 3
Raised edge along truncation. Single line above pearl.

Obv. 4
No raised edge. Single line above coronet pearl.

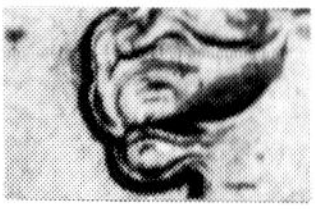

Obv. 5
Raised line around rear curls. Double line above pearl.

No.	Dies[1]	DATE	MINT STATE	E PROOF PLAIN EDGE
2700	**1 A**	**1969**	4.50	
2701	**2 A**	–	2.00	
2702	–	**1970**	4.50	
2703	**4 A**	**1971**		3.00
2704	**4 B**	**1972**		2.50
2705	–	**1974**		2.50
2706	–	**1975**		2.50
2707	**3 A**	**1976**	1.50	
2708	**3 B**	–	9.00	2.00
2709	**4 A**	**1977**	1.25	
2710	**5 B**	–		2.00
2711	**5 A**	**1978**	1.00	
2712	**5 B**	–		2.00
2713	**5 A**	**1979**	.70	
2714	**5 B**	–	4.00	2.00
2715	**5 A**	**1980**	.50	
2716	**5 B**	–		2.50

1: These coins are plain edged.

Note: Small design size variation occurs with decimal issues generally for a specific year.

Des: A.Machin

Obverse 1

Des: D.Wynne

Reverse A

No.	Dies	DATE	MINT STATE	E PROOF PLAIN EDGE
2750	**1 A**	**1973**	1.25	2.50

TEN PENCES

Des: A.Machin

Obverse type

Des: C.Ironside

Reverse type

Obv. 1
'1' of date to space.
'I' right of bead.
'A' left of bead.

Obv. 2
'1' of date r. of bead.
No incuse lines to hair or eyebrow.

Obv. 3
'1' of date r. of bead.
With incuse lines.
'I' to bead.

Obv. 4
'1' of date to space.
'I' left of bead.
'A' to bead.

Obv. 5
'1' of date slightly l. of bead. 'I' r. of bead.
'A' left of bead.

Obv. 6
'1' of date to bead.
'I' left of bead.
'A' right of bead.

Rev. A
'P' of 'Pence' r. of bead. 'E' of 'Pence' left of bead.

Rev. B
'P' of 'Pence' slightly left of bead. 'E' of 'Pence' to space.

Rev. C
'P' of 'Pence' to space.
'E' of 'Pence' to bead.
Legend near border.

Rev. D
'P' of 'Pence' l. of bead.
'E' of 'Pence' r. of bead.
Legend near border.

Rev. E
'P' of 'Pence' r. of bead.
'E' of 'Pence' to bead.
Legend away from border.

Rev. F
'P' of 'Pence' to bead.
'E' of 'Pence' slightly right of bead.

Obv. 7
'1' of date r. of bead. 'A' r. of bead. Hair outline emphasised.

Obv. 9
'1' of date to space. 'A' to space. Bust points to space.

Obv. 8
'1' of date to space. 'A' to space. Bust points to bead.

Obv. 10
'1' of date to bead. 'I' to space. 'A' left of bead.

P

No.	Dies		DATE	MINT STATE	PROOF
2800	**1 A**		**1968**	4.00	
2801	**1 B**		–	*	
2802	**2 A**		–	11.00	
2803	**2 B**		–	.50	
2804	**3 A**		–	.80	
2805	–	Upper rev. beads doubled	–	8.00	
2806	**3 B**		–	.70	
2807	– [2]		**1969**	.60	
2808	**4 B**		**1970**	.70	
2809	**4 F** [1]		–	65.00	
2810	**4 B**		**1971**	.60	2.50
2811	**7 B**		**1972**		3.00
2812	**7 E**		–		2.00
2813	**3 B**		**1973**	.50	3.00
2814	**3 C**		–	85.00	
2815	**3 E**		–		2.00
2816	**4 B**		–	.50	
2817	**5 B**		–	22.00	
2818	**5 C**		–	7.00	
2819	**6 D**		–	35.00	
2820	**9 E**		–		4.50
2821	**3 B**		**1974**	.50	
2822	**7 B**		–		3.00
2823	**7 E**		–		2.00
2824	**4 B**		**1975**	.40	3.00
2825	**4 E**		–	10.00	2.00
2826	**7 B**		**1976**	.30	3.00
2827	**7 E**		–	3.00	2.00
2828	**3 B**		**1977**	.20	
2829	**8 E**		–		3.00
2830	**10 E**		–		2.00
2831	–		**1978**		2.00
2832	**10 B**		**1979**	.15	
2833	**10 E**		–		2.00
2834	**10 B**		**1980**	.10	
2835	**10 E**		–		2.00

1: Also known with severe obv. die crack through front portion of coronet. 2: Known ↑↓.

FIVE PENCES

Des: A.Machin — Des: C.Ironside

Obverse type

Reverse type

Obv. 1
'1' of date to bead. Low outline to rear of hair.

Rev. A
'E' of 'Pence' to space.

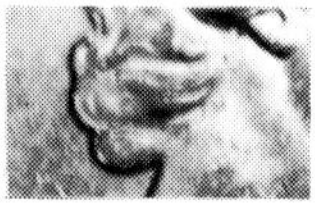

Obv. 2
Hair outline emphasised. 2nd. 'I' of 'II' r. of bead.

Rev. B
'E' of 'Pence' to bead.

Obv. 3
Hair outline emphasised. 2nd. 'I' of 'II' to space.

Obv. 4
'1' of date to space. Legend away from border.

No.	Dies		DATE	MINT STATE	PROOF
2900	**1 A**		**1968**	.25	
2901	–		**1969**	.40	
2902	–		**1970**	.30	
2903	–		**1971**	.50	2.00
2904	–	Broad milling	–	4.50	
2905	**1 B**		**1972**		1.50
2906	**3 B**		**1973**		1.50
2907	**2 B**		**1974**		1.50
2908	**1 A**		**1975**	.25	
2909	**1 B**		–		1.50
2910	**2 B**		**1976**		1.50
2911	**2 A**		**1977**	.15	
2912	**2 B**		–		1.50
2913	**4 B**		–		2.50
2914	**4 A**		**1978**	.10	
2915	**4 B**		–		1.50
2916	**4 A**		**1979**	.05	
2917	**4 B**		–		1.50
2918	**4 A**		**1980**	.05	
2919	**4 B**		–	2.50	1.50

Note: During the mid-seventies some dies were chromium plated to extend their working life. These pieces have a smooth 'glazed' appearance. 25p, 10p & 5p pieces have identical weight, size & composition to previous crowns, florins & shillings.

Proof Sets

Large strikings from specially prepared dies, imparting a mirror-like finish to the coin field. Frosted designs commence 1980. Issued in perspex-type cases with dated medallion. Copper proofs are noted for completeness.

No.	DATE	(£1)	5/-	50p	(20p)	10p	5p	2p	1p	½p	F.D.C. SET £
2960	**1971**			S		M	M	P	P	P	13.00
2961	**1972**		M	S		M	M	P	P	P	13.00
2962	**1973**			S		M	M	P	P	P	9.00
2963	**1974**			S		M	M	P	P	P	8.00
2964	**1975**			S		M	M	P	P	P	7.50
2965	**1976**			S		M	M	P	P	P	8.00
2966	**1977**		M	S		M	M	P	P	P	12.00
2967	**1978**			S		M	M	P	P	P	8.50
2968	**1979**			S		M	M	P	P	P	8.50
2969	**1980**			S		M	M	P	P	P	9.00

M: Milled edge, P: Plain edge, S: Septangular edge, plain.

DECIMAL PATTERNS

The Royal Mint Museum have a number of pattern and trial pieces which remain unpublished, however, these do include two sets, one dated 1961 having values in 'cents' and another dated 1963 with values in 'decimal pence'. The 1961 cupro-nickel coins have designs rendered from previously used puncheons, with the five cent reverse depicting the Royal Cypher from the last issue sixpences of George IV. The ten cent piece adopts the Hanoverian gartered shield from the last issue half-guineas of George III, whilst the twenty cent shows the 'standing Britannia' reverse from the florin of Edward VII. The fifty cent, in silver, adapts a stylised 'Una and the Lion' reverse from Victoria's reign. All these pieces bear Mary Gillick's duodecimal portrait.

The more appropriate 1963 cupro-nickel coins have a five and ten 'decimal pence' of traditional weight and size, with a 'three crowns' and a 'St. George' reverse respectively. A twenty 'decimal pence' coin depicts the Royal Arms within a garter, having supporters, crest and motto. These pieces have Arnold Machin's decimal portrait.

Unofficial Pieces

These pieces, although privately sponsored, reflect contemporary coin design and are frequently collected in conjunction with official issues.

All coins are silver unless stated.

GEORGE III

'Crowns'

No.	Designer	OBV.	REV.	DATE	E PROOF PLAIN EDGE	L LEAD PLAIN EDGE	C Copper PLAIN EDGE	J Copper GILT P.Edge
3000	Mills [1]	Laur. hd,	Cruciform Shields	none	450.00	350.00		
3001	Droz	'Hercules',	Crowned Shield	**1820**	£2100		550.00	750.00

1: for Mudie.

GEORGE IV

'Crowns'

No.	Designer	OBV.	REV.	DATE	E PROOF PLAIN EDGE	G GOLD PLAIN EDGE
3010	Mills [1]	Large bare head,	Royal Arms	**1820**	£2200	£17000
3011	–	– with collar	–	–	£5000	

1: for Whiteaves.

'Halfcrown'

No.	Designer	OBV.	REV.	DATE	E PROOF PLAIN EDGE	C Copper PLAIN EDGE
3020	Binfield	Large laur. head,	'2s6d' laureated	none	720.00	250.00

VICTORIA

'Crowns' Dated 1837

No.	Designer	OBV.	REV.	EDGE	P PROOF	G GOLD	A ALUMINIUM	W HARD WHITE METAL
3030	Bonomi [1]	Coronetted head,	'Britannia'	Plain [2]	450.00	£5000 [4]	140.00	170.00
3031	–	– thick flan	–	– [2]				190.00
						C Copper	L LEAD	WHITE METAL
3032	–	–	–	– [3]		180.00	120.00	140.00
3033	–	– thick flan	–	– [3]				150.00
3034	–	–	–	Milled	580.00	170.00	120.00	140.00
3035	–	–	Royal Arms	Plain	700.00			160.00

1: These intagliated pieces were made in 1893 by J.Rochelle Thomas.

2: Edge numbered.

3: No edge numbering.

4: Weighs 1.285 oz. (equalling five sovereigns).

'Crowns' Dated Mdccclxxxvii (1887)

No.	Designer	OBV.	REV.	EDGE	P PROOF	G GOLD	L LEAD	A ALUMINIUM	R Pewter
3050	Thomas[1]	Ornate bust,	Royal Arms	Plain	500.00				
3051	–	–	, & Spink –	–		£4500	200.00	210.00	220.00
									C Copper
3052	–	–	– –	–					180.00
3053	–	–	– –	Letter[2]	420.00	£4500		210.00	180.00
								W WHITE METAL	T TIN
3054	–	–	– –	–				230.00	240.00
3055	–	–	– –	Milled	500.00	£4500			
3056	–	– 'J.R.T.',[3]	– –	–			210.00		
3057	–	– –	–	Plain	570.00				
3058	–	– 'Spink & Son'[3]	–	–	440.00				

1: for Spink & Son.
2: Reads: 'Made in Bavaria', stamped incuse.
3: On truncation.

No.	Designer	OBV.	REV.	DATE	E PROOF PLAIN EDGE
3070	Kirkwood	Veiled bust,	'Design for a crown piece'	(1894)	£1200

'Halfcrown'

No.	Designer	OBV.	REV.	DATE	Silver Plated P.Edge
3080	P.T.E.	Veiled bust,	Shields & 'model ½crown'	**1890**	320.00

'Shillings'

No.	Designer	OBV.	REV.	DATE	P PROOF	E PROOF PLAIN EDGE	C Copper	CC Copper PLAIN EDGE
3090	Wiener[1]	Crowned bust 'Dei Gra'	Shield	**1863**		120.00		
3091	–	Coron. hd., 'Regina'	–	–		120.00	65.00	60.00
3092	–	– 'Dei Gra'	–	–	160.00	120.00	65.00	
3093	–	Wreathed hd., –	–	–		120.00		60.00
3094	–	Coron. hd., 'CW'[2] –	–	**1865**		120.00		60.00
3095	–	Wreathed hd. – –	–	–		120.00		60.00
3096	–	– – 'Regina'	–	–		120.00	65.00	60.00
3097	–	Coron. hd. 'Dei Gra', Gartered	–	none		100.00		50.00
3098	–	Wreathed hd. –	–	–		100.00		50.00
3099	–	Coron. hd. 'Regina'	–	–		100.00		50.00
3100	–	– 'Dei Gra', no legend	–	–	120.00	105.00		
3101	–	Wreathed hd. – , with motto	–	–		150.00		
3102	–	Coron. hd. 'Regina',	'One shilling'	–		150.00		
3103	–	– 'CHW'[2] 'Dei Gra',	–	–		150.00		

1: Reverses by W.J.Taylor. 2: On truncation.
Note: 'Wiener' pieces muled with official dies are numbers 961 to 964.

'Sixpences' Dated Mdccclxxxvii (1887)

No.	Designer	OBV.	REV.	EDGE	P PROOF	G GOLD	C Copper	A ALUMINIUM	T TIN
3120	Thomas[1]	Ornate bust,	Royal Arms	Plain	80.00				
3121	–	–	'Spink & Son' –	–		520.00	60.00	55.00	
3122	–	–	–	Letter[2]	85.00	540.00	60.00	55.00	65.00
									X BRASS
3123	–	–	–	Milled	80.00	540.00	60.00		50.00

1: for Spink & Son. These pieces would correspond to their crown-size issues.
2: Reads: 'Made in Bavaria', stamped incuse.

EDWARD VII

'Crowns'

No.	Designer	OBV.	REV.	DATE	P PROOF PLAIN EDGE	G GOLD PLAIN EDGE
3140	Spink[1]	King on horseback,	Garnished shield	**1902**	550.00	£4500
3141	–	– double flan	–	–	800.00	
3142	–	– quadruple flan	–	–	950.00	

1: These pieces are 13½% heavier than official weight.

GEORGE V

'Crowns' Dated 1910

No.	Designer	OBV.	REV.	EDGE	P PROOF	M MATT PROOF	G GOLD	C Copper	Y Copper Plated
3150	A.Wyon	Bare hd.dated,	'St.George'	Plain	£1700[1]	£1200	£8500	600.00	950.00
3151	–	–	–	Milled	£1800[2]	£1300[3]	£9000		
3152	–	Bare hd,	'St.George & date'	–	£1800	£1400[1]	£9000		
3153	–	– heavy flan	–	–	£2000[4]				
3154	–	–	–	Plain	£1900[4]		£8500	600.00	

1: Lighter than official weight (.88 oz.).
2: Weighs 1 oz.
3: In pure silver (.999).
4: Weighs 1.05 oz.

'Doubleflorins'

No.	Designer	OBV.	REV.	DATE	P PROOF	E PROOF PLAIN EDGE	Q ANGLESY[1] Copper	H Cornish Copper, P.Edge[1]	F PHOS. Bronze P.Edge[1]
3170	R.Huth	Draped bust,	Shields no val.	**1911**	600.00	620.00	160.00[2]	160.00	160.00
									I IRON[1]
3171	–	– ,	'Rex-bri' & value	–					200.00[3]
								N NICKEL[1] P.Edge	Z ZINC[1] P.Edge
3172	–	– ,	'Bri-rex' & value	–	600.00	620.00		180.00	170.00[4]

1: Metal name stamped on obv. field.
2: With incuse edge: 'On Demand in London Liverpool or Anglesy'.
3: With incuse edge: 'Ships Nails Calshot Castle May 1896' & weighs .87 oz.
4: Weighs 1.285 oz. (equalling five sovereigns).

					P	E	G	U	N
No.	Designer	OBV.	REV.	DATE	PROOF	PROOF PLAIN EDGE	GOLD PLAIN EDGE	PLAT INUM P.Edge	NICKEL PLAIN EDGE
3190	R.Huth	Draped bust,	'12 groats'	**1914**	650.00	620.00	£2800	£3800	170.00
3191	—	'Rex-bri' & value,	—	**11& 14**		260.00 [1]			

1: A mule of 1911 & 1914 reverses.

'Eightpences'

					P	G	U	N	C
No.	Designer	OBV.	REV.	DATE	PROOF	GOLD	PLAT INUM	NICKEL	Copper
3200	R.Huth	Draped bust,	'Octorino'	**1913**	180.00	750.00	700.00	80.00	60.00
3201	—	—	'Eightpence'	—	180.00	750.00	700.00	80.00	60.00

APPENDIX I

Official Coinage Weights and Finenesses

DENOMINATION	PERIOD	Dia-meter m.m.	MINT WEIGHT GRAMS	MINT WEIGHT [1] TROY	SILVER FINE-NESS	Bullion content @ £5 oz	Cu.Ni. £1500 per ton [2]
Crown	1818 – 1902	38	436.36	.909	.925	£4.20	
—	1927 – 1937	—	—	—	.500	£2.27	
—	1951 – 1965	—	—	—	CuNi		4p
Double Florin	1887 – 1890	36	349.09	.727	.925	£3.36	
Halfcrown	1816 – 1919	32	218.18	.454	—	£2.10	
—	1920 – 1946	—	—	—	.500	£1.14	
—	1947 – 1970	—	—	—	CuNi		2p
Florin [3]	1849 – 1919		174.54	.363	.925	£1.68	
—	1920 – 1946	28	—	—	.500	£1.14	
—	1947 – 1970	—	—	—	CuNi		1.6p
Shilling	1816 – 1919	23	87.27	.181	.925	.84	
—	1920 – 1946	—	—	—	.500	.45	
—	1947 – 1970	—	—	—	CuNi		.8p
Sixpence	1816 – 1920	19	43.63	.090	.925	.42	
—	1920 – 1946	—	—	—	.500	.23	
—	1947 – 1970	—	—	—	CuNi		.4p
Groat	1836 – 1888	16	29.09	.060	.925	.28	
Threepence	1834 – 1920	—	21.81	.045	—	.21	
—	1920 – 1944	—	—	—	.500	.11	
Twopence	1838 – 1848	13	14.54	.030	.925	.14	
Threehalfpence	1834 – 1862	12	10.90	.022	—	.10	
Maundy Set [4]	1817 – 1920		72.73	.151	—	.70	
—	1921 – 1946		—	—	.500	.38	
—	1947 – 1970		—	—	.925	.70	

1: Circulated silver averages 3½% lighter weight.
2: Cupro-nickel: 75% copper 25% nickel.
3: Four flan sizes occur: 1849 27¾ mm, 1851—1887 Gothic 30mm, 1887 —1892 Jubilee 29mm, 1893—1970 28mm.
4: Comprises 4d, 3d, 2d & 1d.

APPENDIX II

Duodecimal Currency Tables

The following tables illustrate the quantity of coin issued each year per denomination. Generally speaking this represents all those coins bearing that particular date, but this is not always correct and figures known to be illogical have been readjusted. Maundy figures indicate the maximum complete sets struck in thousands, whilst other denominations are noted in millions. Currency twopence mintages are to be confirmed.

DATE	5/-	2/6	2/-	1/-	6d	4d	3d	1½d	Mau.set
1816		8.093		23.031	10.922				
1817									2,970
1818	.155	2.905		1.342	4.285				1,980
1819	.683	4.790		7.595	4.712				
1820	.448	2.397		7.975	1.489				1,980
1821	.438	1.435		2.463	.863				
1822	.125								2,970
1823		2.004		.693					1,980
1824		.466		4.158	.634				1,584
1825		2.259		2.459	.483				2,376
1826		2.189		6.352	.689				2,376
1827				.574	.166				2,772
1828		.050			.016				2,772
1829		.508		.879	.404				2,772
1830									2,772
1831					1.340				3,564
1832									2,574
1833									2,574
1834		.993		3.223	5.892		.401	.800	2,574
1835		.282		1.449	1.552		.491	.634	2,574
1836		1.589		3.568	1.988	4.253	.412	.158	2,574
1837		.151		.479	.507	.962	.943	.031	2,574
1838				1.956	1.608	2.150	1.204	.539	4,158
1839				5.667	3.311	1.461	.570	.760	4,125
1840		.386		1.639	2.099	1.497	.634	.095	4,125
1841		.043		.873	1.386	.345	.444	.158	2,574
1842		.486		2.095	.602	.725		1.869	4,125
1843		.455		1.465	3.160	1.818	2.028	.475	4,158
1844	.159	1.999		4.467	3.976	.855	1.045		4,158
1845	.235	2.232		4.083	3.719	.915	1.315		4,158
1846		1.540		4.031	4.269	1.366	.048		4,158
1847	.068					.226			4,158
1848		.459		1.041	.586	.713			4,158
1849		.261	.414	.645		.380	.127		4,158
1850		.485		.685	.705		.950		4,158
1851				.470	2.288	.594	.479		4,158
1852			1.016	1.307	.905	.031			4,158
1853			3.920	4.256	3.838	.012	.032		4,158
1854			.550	.552	.840	1.097	1.467		4,158
1855			.831	1.368	1.129	.741	.383		4,158
1856			2.202	3.168	2.780		1.914		4,158
1857			1.671	2.562	2.233		1.758		4,158
1858			2.239	3.109	1.932		1.441		4,158
1859			2.568	4.562	4.689		3.580		4,158
1860			1.475	1.671	1.703		3.406	.160	4,158
1861				1.382			3.295		4,158
1862			.594	.954	.990		1.156	.256	4,158
1863			.939	.859	.491		.950		4,158
1864			1.861	4.518	4.253		1.331		4,158
1865			1.580	5.619	1.632		1.742		4,158
1866			.915	4.990	5.140		1.901		4,158
1867			.424	2.166	1.362		.713		4,158
1868			.897	3.330	1.069		1.457		4,158
1869			.297	.737	.388		?		4,158

APPENDIX II

DATE	5/-	4/-	2/6	2/-	1/-	6d	4d	3d	Mau.set
1870				1.981	1.467	.480		1.284	4,488
1871				3.426	4.910	3.663		1.000	4,488
1872				7.200	8.898	3.382		1.293	4,328
1873				5.922	6.490	4.595		4.056	4,162
1874			2.189	1.643	5.504	4.226		4.427	4,488
1875			1.113	1.117	4.354	3.257		3.306	4,154
1876			.633	.580	1.057	.841		1.834	4,488
1877			.447	.682	2.981	4.066		2.622	4,488
1878			1.466	1.787	3.127	2.625		2.420	4,488
1879			.901	1.512	3.612	3.326		3.140	4,488
1880			1.346	2.167	4.843	3.893		1.610	4,488
1881			2.301	2.570	5.255	6.239		3.248	4,488
1882			.808		1.612	.760		.473	4,146
1883			2.983	3.556	7.281	4.987		4.370	4,488
1884			1.569	1.447	3.924	3.423		3.322	4,488
1885			1.628	1.758	3.337	4.653		5.184	4,488
1886			.892	.592	2.087	2.728		6.153	4,488
1887Y			.262	.544	.603	1.612		1.763	4,488
- J	.274	.483	1.176	1.233	3.431	2.064		1.022	
1888	.132	.243	1.429	1.548	4.527	4.198	.120	.518	4,488
1889	1.807	1.185	4.812	2.974	7.040	8.739		4.587	4,488
1890	.998	.782	3.228	1.685	8.794	9.387		4.466	4,488
1891	.566		2.285	.836	5.665	7.023		6.323	4,488
1892	.451		1.711	.283	4.592	6.246		2.578	4,488
1893J						.341		1.315	
- O	.498		1.793	1.666	7.039	7.010		1.762	8,976
1894	.145		1.525	1.953	5.953	3.468		1.609	8,976
1895	.253		1.773	2.183	8.881	7.025		4.789	8,877
1896	.318		2.149	2.944	9.265	6.652		4.598	8,476
1897	.262		1.679	1.700	6.270	5.031		4.541	8,976
1898	.161		1.870	3.061	9.769	5.914		4.597	8,976
1899	.166		2.864	3.997	10.965	7.997		6.246	8,976
1900	.353		4.479	5.529	10.938	8.984		10.644	8,976
1901			1.557	2.649	3.426	5.109		6.098	8,976
1902	.256		1.316	2.190	7.809	6.367		8.268	8,976
1903			.275	1.995	2.062	5.410		5.227	8,976
1904			.710	2.770	2.040	4.487		3.627	8,976
1905			.166	1.188	.488	4.236		3.548	8,976
1906			2.886	6.910	10.791	7.641		3.152	8,800
1907			3.694	5.948	14.083	8.734		4.831	8,760
1908			1.759	3.280	3.807	6.739		8.158	8,760
1909			3.052	3.483	5.665	6.584		4.055	1,983
1910			2.558	5.651	26.547	12.491		4.563	1,440
1911			2.915	5.951	20.066	9.155		5.841	1,635
1912			4.701	8.572	15.594	10.984		8.933	1,246
1913			4.090	4.545	9.012	7.500		7.143	1,228
1914			18.333	21.253	23.416	22.715		6.734	982
1915			32.433	12.368	39.279	15.695		5.451	1,293
1916			29.530	21.064	35.862	22.207		18.555	1,128
1917			11.172	11.182	22.203	7.725		21.662	1,237
1918			29.080	29.212	34.916	27.559		20.631	1,375
1919			10.267	9.469	10.824	13.375		16.846	1,258
1920			17.982	15.388	22.825	14.136		16.704	1,399
1921			23.678	34.864	22.649	30.340		8.749	1,386
1922			16.397	23.861	27.216	16.879		7.980	1,373
1923			26.309	21,547	14.575	6.383			1,430
1924			5.866	4.582	9.250	17.444			1,515
1925			1.413	1,404	5.419	12.721		3.732	1,438
1926			4.474	5.242	22.516	21.810		4.108	1,504
1927			6.826		9.262	8.940			1,647
1928	.009		18.763	11.087	18.137	23.123		1.302	1,642
1929	.005		17.633	16.397	19.343	28.319			1,761
1930	.005		.809	5.754	3.137	16.990		1.319	1,724

DATE	5/-	2/6	2/-	1/-E	1/-S	6d	3d	Mau.set
1931	.004	11.264	6.556	6.994		16.873	6.252	1,759
1932	.002	4.794	.717	12.168		9.406	5.887	1,835
1933	.007	10.311	8.685	11.512		22.185	5.579	1,872
1934	.001	2.422		6.138		9.304	7.406	1,887
1935	.712	7.022	7.541	9.183		13.996	7.028	1,928
1936	.002	7.039	9.897	11.911		24.380	3.239	1,307
1937	.419	9.106	13.007	8.359	6.749	22.303	8.148	1,325
1938		6.426	7.909	4.833	4.798	13.403	6.402	1,275
1939		15.479	20.851	11.053	10.264	28.670	1.356	1,234
1940		17.948	18.700	11.099	9.913	20.875	7.914	1,277
1941		15.774	24.451	11.392	8.086	23.087	7.979	1,253
1942		31.220	39.895	17.454	13.677	44.943	4.144	1,231
1943		15.463	26.712	11.404	9.824	46.927	1.379	1,239
1944		15.255	27.560	11.587	10.990	37.953	2.006	1,259
1945		19.849	25.858	15.143	15.106	39.939		1,355
1946		22.725	22.300	18.664	16.382	43.466		1,365
1947		21.910	22.910	12.121	12.283	29.993		1,375
1948		71.165	67.554	45.577	45.352	88.324		1,385
1949		28.273	28.615	19.328	21.243	41.356		1,395
1950		28.336	24.357	19.244	14.300	32.742		1,405
1951		9.004	27.412	9.957	10.961	40.399		1,468
1952						1.013		1,012
1953	5.963	3.883	11.959	41.943	20.664	70.324		1,025
1954		11.615	13.085	30.262	26.772	105.241		1,020
1955		23.629	25.887	45.260	27.951	109.930		1,036
1956		33.935	47.825	44.907	42.854	109.842		1,088
1957		34.201	33.071	42.774	17.960	105.654		1,094
1958		15.746	9.565	14.392	40.823	123.519		1,100
1959		9.029	14.080	19.443	1.013	93.089		1,106
1960	1.024	19.929	13.832	27.028	14.377	103.288		1,112
1961		25.888	37.735	39.817	2.763	115.052		1,118
1962		24.013	35.148	36.404	18.967	166.484		1,125
1963		17.635	26.471	49.743	32.309	120.056		1,131
1964		5.973	16.539	8.591	5.239	152.336		1,137
1965	19.640	9.879	48.163	9.216	2.774	127.872		1,143
1966		11.583	83.999	15.005	15.607	171.636		1,206
1967		33.058	39.718			240.788		986

Duodecimal Proof Tables

DATE	5/-	4/-	2/6	2/-	1/-E	1/-S	6d	4d	3d	Mau.set
1826	350		400		400		450			
1831	150		400		250		450			300
1839	350		400		350		350	350		350
1847	8,000[1]									
1853	80		100	100	120		150	200		220
1887	1,084	1,084	1,084	1,084	1,084		1,084		1,084	
1893	1,329		1,329	1,329	1,329		1,329		1,329	
1902	15,123		15,123	15,123	15,123		15,123			15,123
1911			6,007	6,007	6,007		6,007			6,007
1927	15,030		15,022	15,022	15,022		15,022		15,022	
1935	2,500[2]									
1937	26,402		26,402	26,402	26,402	26,402	26,402		26,402	26,402
1950			17,513	17,513	17,513	17,513	17,513			
1951	2.004		20,000	20,000	20,000	20,000	20,000			
1953	40,000		40,000	40,000	40,000	40,000	40,000			
1970			.750	.750	.750	.750	.750			

1: 'Gothic' issue.
2: Raised edge issue.
Note: 1826, 1831, 1839 & 1853 mintage figures are estimates.

APPENDIX III

Latin and Other Legends on Tower Hill Coins

Latin etc. *phrase*	English *translation*
Anno Regni	*In the year of our reign.*
Britt: Omn: Rex (Regina) Fid: Def: Ind: Imp: (also Brit: Britanniar: Britanniarum)	*King (Queen) of all the Britons, Defender of the faith, Emperor (Empress) of India.*
Civium Industria Floret Civitas	*By the industry of its people the State flourishes.*
Decus et Tutamen	*A decoration and a safeguard.*
Dei Gratia	*By the grace of God.*
Dieu et Mon Droit	*My God and my right.*
Dirige (Dirigit) Deus Gressus Meos	*May the Lord guide my footsteps.*
Foedus Inviolabile	*An unviolable treaty.*
Honi Soit qui Mal y Pense	*Evil unto him who thinks evil.*
Incorrupta Fides Veritasque	*A pure and righteous faith.*
Tueatur Unita Deus	*May God protect this unity.*

Numerical Translations

Secundo	*Second*
Tertio	*Third*
Septimo	*Seventh*
Octavo	*Eighth*
Nono	*Ninth*
Undecimo	*Eleventh*
Decimo Septimo	*Seventeenth*
Quinquagesimo Septimo	*Fifty-seventh*

APPENDIX IV

Select Bibliography

Craig,	Sir John	*The Mint*	Cambridge 1953
Linecar, Stone,	H.W.A. & A.G.	*English Proof and Pattern Crown-size pieces.*	London 1968
Royal Mint		*Annual Report of the Deputy Master and Comptroller*	London
Seaby,	H.A.	*The English Silver Coinage from 1649.*	London 1974
Seaby,	P.S. & H.A.	*Coins of England.*	London 1980